Mass Media in a Free Society

Mass Media in a Free Society

**Edited by
Warren K. Agee**

The University Press of Kansas

Lawrence | Manhattan
Wichita | London

Preface

Six mass media specialists, widely known for their professional stature and insightful minds, were asked to explore in depth the issues raised by the vexing problems of communication and understanding in a mass society. What were their analyses and predictions, their hopes and fears, and their thoughtful estimates of the adjustments that the media must make to help keep our democratic society viable and strong in a rapidly moving world?

The William Allen White Centennial Seminar, conducted at the University of Kansas in 1968, constituted an appropriate tribute to the famous Emporia (Kansas) *Gazette* editor, statesman, and world citizen, who died in 1944. The six key lecturers, together with almost a dozen other outstanding mass communications critic-commentators, gathered for three days to discuss how, as columnist Carl Rowan put it, "through the press and the tube we can mobilize in our generation some of the wisdom and compassion that were the mark of William Allen White . . . [and] to explore means through which some of us may serve as true citizens of our towns and our world and leave on them the same marks of courage and insight that William Allen White left on his town and his times."

Press critic Ben Bagdikian expounded one of the principal themes when he called on the news media to do a better job in detecting early breakdowns in the social system and in providing systematic information so the public might decide upon a course of action. "We need a systematic collection of expert presentations of solutions to leading problems, expressed clearly and fairly," Bagdikian stated. "There should be a variety of these, attempting to cover the whole spectrum of ideas whether or not these ideas agree with the opinions of the news proprietor or with his professionals. This requires journalists who are in constant touch with the world of scholarship and of social action. It requires proprietors who permit presentation of these ideas based on professional and not partisan judgment. It could be the greatest contribution the news media of this country could make to the reservoir of ideas from which public understanding and public policy can find solutions to problems."

Associated Press news executive Samuel Blackman contended that newspapers already are providing much of this expert information, citing as examples articles written by such historians as Allan Nevins and Daniel Boorstin. He disputed Bagdikian's conclusion that local newspaper coverage is too largely of the "cops-tag-overtime-parkers" variety. The newspapers, he said, "are looking at pollution of water, air, and the minds of the young; at poverty and its causes; at the phenomenon of a generation of youngsters impatient with all standards; at the generation of women emancipated by the pill; and at churches in the midst of revolt."

Norman Isaacs, executive editor of the Louis-ville *Courier-Journal* and *Times,* agreed with Bagdikian that press performance is "too often pretty shoddy." In Isaacs's mind, "editors ought to still be rebels, part wild men, not only taking on the Establishment but taking it apart." The future of journalism, he stated, "must be built on a parity with the academic community, in which the young man or woman who goes into journalism will look on it in terms of having economic and status equality with that of the academic world. And when we get to that point we shall have built a partnership between these two great institutions."

Hodding Carter, Pulitzer Prize-winning editor and publisher of the *Delta Democrat-Times,* Greenville, Mississippi, agreed that newspapers must be deeply committed to a set of social values that transcend private interest. "Our responsibility," he said, "is to keep people informed to the best of our ability, to make people ashamed, to make people proud, and to help keep people free."

Another prize-winning journalist, Houstoun Waring, editor emeritus of the Littleton *Independent* and Arapahoe *Herald*, Littleton, Colorado, defended editors and publishers as being not menial, but lacking specialized knowledge of many fields. He agreed with Bagdikian that the practice of printing articles by experts should be greatly increased, "especially in the realm of economics, which has largely been left to the magazines."

Ben Hibbs, retired editor of the *Saturday Evening Post* and now a contributing editor to *Reader's Digest*, expressed the opinion that magazines generally are doing a competent job in acquainting citizens with, and suggesting solutions to, the perplexing problems of our times.

Bill D. Moyers, former presidential press secretary and now publisher of *Newsday* on Long Island, New York, said he had learned at the White House that "of all the great myths of American journalism, objectivity is the greatest." He thus echoed Rowan's admission that "what we say to our readers, and how we say it, is surely conditioned by our own ideologies, our own notions about what ought to be the shape of future world society." Moyers called on journalists to act with the same appreciation of candor about themselves that they expect of public officials. "This," he said, "would lead to several improvements: An admission of the subjectivity of our objectivity; a confession that not even the press can discover the 'whole truth and nothing but the truth'—that at best we can only come up with the 'bits and pieces of truth'; and an acknowledgment that our responsibility is greater than the skill with which we pretend to discharge it."

Asserting that a serious "credibility gap" now exists between the press and the people as well as between government and the people, Moyers said there is considerable public skepticism about the "cozy ties" between the press and government at every level, "and much of this skepticism is justified." He said the press should take steps to avoid both the appearance and the actuality of a liaison with government, "for the press and the government are not allies—they are adversaries. . . . . How each performs is crucial to the workings of a system that is both free and open but fallible and fragile . . . Each of us must guard against poorly formed judgments about the other and against an unperturbable sense of security about our own well-being."

Asking "Where has the press been all this time?", Rowan deplored what he termed the provincial philosophy of many newspapers and their failure for decades to alert citizens to America's growing race problem. Both he and Theodore Koop, vice-president of the Columbia Broadcasting System, called for "minimal exposure" of the Stokely Carmichaels and the Rap Browns. Instead, said Rowan, "if reason is not to fail men in our time, we of the press must give men the information, the knowledge, to sustain reason. We can do so by practicing the journalism of hope—and I do not mean a journalism that offers only the pre-sweetened pap of empty optimism. We can tell our readers the hard truths, the grim realities, and still have it add up to constructive journalism."

Koop said that in only twenty years television has reshaped the entire communications process and earned the accolade of being America's "star reporter" by virtue of the dependence for news which most Americans have placed upon the industry. In covering the Vietnam war, Koop stated, "television has banished the glamor of war forever." A dilemma still exists, however, in reporting an urban riot without generating further violence, Koop pointed out. With maturity, he said, television and radio should become bolder in their editorial statements and thus help to provide a greater variety of community voices, both editorial and news. Koop predicted "a marked increase in news and public affairs programs beyond the 20 to 25 per cent of current network scheduling." Satellite television, he declared, can become an open world "hot line" for all peoples to see and hear and share—and hopefully understand.

Stan Freberg, advertising executive and satirist, excoriated much television advertising as being mediocre, dull, insipid, nauseating, and irritating, and an insult to the viewer's intelligence. Deploring the quality of both the programming and the commercials, he set forth "The Freberg Part-time Television Plan," described as "a startling, but perfectly reasonable proposal for the de-escalation of television in a free society, mass media-wise." In an exchange with Koop after the latter's lecture, Freberg in effect dared the Columbia Broadcasting System to employ him as a satirist to follow network newscasts and set the news in honest, humorous perspective.

In closing the seminar series, Bosley Crowther, longtime movie critic of the New York *Times,* underscored the contention of some previous speakers that the mass media had failed to prepare the American public to meet many of its present problems. "War films of the past have not prepared us for revulsion to the war in Vietnam," Crowther stated. "Neither have movies shown us, except in a few documentaries of late and in one or two minor feature pictures, the immensity and the tragedy of the long drama of racial injustice that has been occurring in our midst." Deploring excessive violence in many movies today, Crowther questioned whether such films accurately reflect "the larger public sense of rightness and desirability." He foresaw no overall improvement in movie culture. "Perhaps," he said, "we may have to undergo some terrible passage through a valley of social strife, some further upheaval, before we or our children witness an essential change in the culture of films."

The total length of the seminar discussions, which consumed almost fifteen hours, precludes the inclusion of the remarks of the critic-commentators in this book, beyond those salient points covered in this preface. Commentaries one hour or longer accompanied each lecture. Audio tapes of each of the sessions may be obtained from the William Allen White School of Journalism, University of Kansas, Lawrence. Critic-commentators not previously named were Grover Cobb, chairman of the board, National Association of Broadcasters, and vice-president, station KVGB, Great Bend, Kansas; Irving Dilliard, former editorial editor, St. Louis *Post-Dispatch,* and now a visiting professor at Princeton University; Richard Dodderidge, partner, Bruce B. Brewer Company, Inc., Kansas City, Missouri (advertising); and Ernest K. Lindley, special assistant, Secretary of State, and former chief, Washington Bureau of *Newsweek.* The tapes also include the remarks of the moderators: Dolph C. Simons, Jr., publisher, Lawrence (Kansas) *Daily Journal-World;* Bill Vaughan, columnist, Kansas City *Star;* Tom Kiene, managing editor, Topeka (Kansas) *Capital-Journal;* John Colburn, editor and publisher, Wichita (Kansas) *Eagle* and *Beacon;* Arthur Wolf, co-owner, Centron Corporation, Inc., Lawrence (film); and Cobb. Whitley Austin, editor, Salina (Kansas) *Journal,* moderated a closing dinner discussion.

The William Allen White Foundation and the William Allen White School of Journalism at the University jointly sponsored the seminar, one of a series of year-long events commemorating the hundredth birthday of White.

The foundation extends thanks to the scores of individuals and organizations which contributed funds to underwrite the centennial activities. The writer extends special thanks to the foundation trustees, to members of the university-wide co-ordinating committee, to the school's faculty members, and to others who worked tirelessly in behalf of the year's activities.

Warren K. Agee
Dean, William Allen White School of Journalism
Director, William Allen White Foundation

February, 1969

Contents

Mass Media in a Free Society

Ben H. Bagdikian
The Press and Its Crisis
of Identity

I have been told that my job is to summarize what seems to me to be the state of the American press. This requires a combination of arrogance and compassion. The arrogance allows me to generalize about 1,700 daily newspapers, 9,500 weeklies, 9,000 periodicals, and 7,000 broadcasting stations, most of which I have never seen or heard. The compassion goes out to the news media which have a similarly impossible assignment to inform the citizen each day about the state of his fellow three billion human beings, most of whom have not been seen, either. Perhaps the press and its observers can join in the common sin of seeing little and talking much.

We do this in the name of William Allen White, who is an instructive model of how to learn something universal from the fragment that represents one man's life. He was born a hundred years ago, and he lived and worked in a small town on a tiny paper. Yet when he died twenty-four years ago he had made a lasting impression on American journalism and on American life. He did it by sharing, to use Justice Holmes's phrase, the action and passion of his times.

He was a newspaper publisher and a Republican, not a rare combination. But he had a rare attitude. He was irreverent about the journalistic and political rituals of his time, but he was reverent about their being put to high human purpose.

We ask practitioners and proprietors of news institutions to devote themselves to high human purpose, in other words, to be committed men. But committed to what? In the past, on large political issues most of the news media that expressed their opinions have been overwhelmingly of the same opinion. In an era of monopoly, what if they do that now? And what if they are wrong? We can doubt the universal wisdom of all journalists, even including ourselves, without doubting their sincerity. They can be sincerely wrong. The sad fact is that not all men who find themselves in important positions in the news are wise and humane. William Allen Whites don't grow on trees, though some of his more excitable readers were ready to try the experiment.

It is appropriate that we raise the question of the press's commitment on the William Allen White Centennial. During his last years, White feared that Hitler would destroy all democracy and that the United States would not move soon enough to prevent it.

He lived in a crisis for his country and felt obligated to do something about it.

One generation later we face another crisis in this country, worse, I think, than the depression of the 1930's, worse than World War II, and worse than the destructive hysteria of the early 1950's. We are teetering on the edge of urban civil war and race conflict, whose signs in burned cities, mutual fears, and ethnic suicide are unmistakable.

In the years after the crash of 1929 we also suffered panic and anarchy. Fear and violence broke out all over the country. Some hated the Jews. The farmers hated the bankers. The Marxists and many others hated the capitalistic system. Many rioted. We never found, during the 1930's, a permanent cure for the economic depression, but we did find a way to restore confidence in the governmental system by making a significant improvement in the lives of the citizens. But what if the antagonists at that time had been identifiable by color, and if they had been united whether they liked it or not in clearly different sections of every city?

Had we lost World War II, American democracy obviously would have been suppressed for most of our lives. Yet, we did not panic because hardly any of us doubted that we would eventually win. We were convinced that a democratic system could manage the crisis, and it did.

Had the McCarthyist hysteria of the 1950's prevailed, it would have destroyed the rule of reason and justice. But its most noticeable actor was capricious, finally attacking people and institutions, like the armed services and the President, that even the most frightened Americans knew were not treasonous.

Today our cities are in peril, not in any subtle or distant way, but violently and immediately. Great metropolitan centers are gutted by fire. A large minority of Americans is compacted in their ghettos and, after failure to break out by every other means, is burning them down, committing a kind of group suicide, calling out, as do most would-be suicides, for help that does not come any other way. This is the most urgent symptom of other profound ills, of chaos in the rest of the metropolis, of increasing failure of much public education, and upheavals in rural life.

The greatest danger in our present urban crisis is the doubt that these ills can be remedied by democratic and civilized means.

Any study of our history tells us that it is possible. But it is not certain that it will be.

What should we expect of our news institutions in such a time? Should they merely record what they see? Or should they do something more about changing it? Confronted with these conflicting challenges, most news institutions have emulated the foreman who, when asked by the judge for the jury's verdict, replied, "Your honor, we decided not to get involved."

The crisis in our urban society is matched by a time of choice among our news institutions. The fact is that their environment has been changing faster than they have. A different population has new needs and requires changed journalistic forms. Yet few organizations have evolved them.

It is not enough to point to the best work of the best newspapers and broadcast stations. A better test is to take a 300-mile drive in any part of the country. Pick up every newspaper published within ten miles of the highway. Listen to every radio station receivable along the way. Then characterize their average contribution to the well-being of their communities. I do not recommend this for anyone susceptible to extreme depression.

One press critic took a more daring approach. Irving Kristol, referring to American journalism as "The Underdeveloped Profession," took one of the best papers, the New York *Times,* and said that if all papers are as good as that they are terrible.

I don't share Kristol's perspective. He seems to be arguing for an elitist newspaper everywhere, written by intellectuals only for intellectuals. He seemed to have his eye only on the *Times,* the *Wall Street Journal,* and the *Christian Science Monitor,* the closest we have to national newspapers, reaching only 3 per cent of the readers, and those in a narrow band across the whole country. The other 1,746 papers are local papers and presume to speak to their whole community, not just of the gold crisis but of the P.T.A. meeting, not just to faculty members but to their janitors, not just to adults with their fixed reading habits but to their children whose reading habits are being formed.

But Kristol put his finger on a central failing of the contemporary press when he said that most news organizations confuse judgment and prejudice, that they decide not to get involved in making judgments about the news because they fear the result of personal prejudice by the reporter or editor. He wrote: "The commitment to so-called 'objective' and impersonal reporting of 'spot news' is, in practice, a rationalization for 'safe' and mindless reporting. To keep a reporter's prejudices out of a story is commendable; to keep his judgment out of a story is to guarantee that truth will be emasculated."

Journalism has always been an exercise in judgment. We all see much more than we can possibly report; what we see depends a great deal on what we are. We need to judge what is important and then describe what is important without bias. But the doctrine of objectivity too often has been used as an excuse to avoid conscious and rational decisions which are nevertheless made one way or another anyway. A paper may report objectively that the police are not tagging overtime parkers, and this may be honestly described. But if this is the extent of a paper's examination of its city, then it is obvious that no editor or reporter has objectively reviewed what other community issues may be more important.

This kind of judgment is needed more than ever. It used to be slovenly to pass on every indiscriminate bit of information that came into the newsroom. It is now impossible. Modern communications media are flooding us with words and ideas, and the flow will get more copious. Scholarly information doubles every twelve years. Something like this is happening in the news network. Cables that used to transmit sixty words a minute now do 1,200 words a minute. Speed is impersonal. The machines don't care whether they are transmitting truth or falsity. Error is more efficient than ever.

So whether news organizations like it or not, they have to get "involved" in ways that were considered unobjective a few years ago. The pressure will increase each year to select, analyze, and synthesize, and this means the application of social values. This means that the journalist's belief, as well as the facts he observes, will be important to public attitudes.

There are signs that this new pressure is reaching a point of conflict with contemporary conventions of news. Wire services are always being told to tell the reader the meaning of the news. Broadcasters are asked to get behind the surface events. Yet the customers often rebel when they disagree with the meanings. In a number of newspapers in recent months—in San Francisco, Philadelphia, Providence, and Louisville—there have been open disputes on editorial policy between publishers and working professionals. These and many other signs tell us that the press has not satisfactorily solved its crisis of identity.

These conflicting identities are real.

The newspaper business is a great, clanking industry that buys paper at seven cents a pound and sells it at thirty-six. Television owners purchase a license from the government for $33.33 a year and sell the results for as much as $10 million. They are corporations dedicated to profit.

At the same time, they are also educational institutions which subscribe to canons of professionalism that promise public service before anything else, including, by implication, profits. They do more education of juveniles and adults, in per capita hours of exposure, than do the schools.

The proprietor of a news medium is traditionally supposed to take a personal stand on public issues, in the editorial, based on his own values and institutional responsibility. Yet, the same man is also asked to give independence to a staff of professional journalists whose knowledge of the issues is supposed to be better than his. Does the proprietor repress his own honest feelings and submit to a group decision of his professionals?

And what about group decisions of professional journalists? Such men are supposed to be well-informed, but on any given issue there are many experts who know infinitely more and have gone more deeply into the subject. Does the journalist still express his own personal feelings? Or does he repress these and present some homogenized opinion of the experts? And, finally, if the journalist defers to the experts in deciding the editorial stand of his paper, to which expert does he defer, given the wide differences of the experts on almost any subject?

I think these conflicts of identity will always exist because there are no doctrinaire answers.

For example, a profitless paper will soon die; a losing broadcast station will fall silent or be sold. Yet, a news medium without constructive social purpose might as well be dead. The problem today is not that this tension between profit and public service exists, but that so much of corporate journalism pretends that it does not. It is considered bad taste to talk publicly about the fact that the primary source of our political and social intelligence is a set of corporations in business to make money. It is refreshing to hear Lord Thomson and Cecil Harmsworth King boasting that they are in journalism for profit. It's not always so refreshing to see how they do it. So, without urging emulation of the average newspaper of Lord Thomson or Mr. King, I would urge emulation of their lack of guilt. The issue is not how much money a man makes in journalism, it is what kind of journalism he produces.

We would all be better off if more news proprietors were better businessmen, if they knew more about themselves and were less devoted to hearing only happy things about themselves, told by the astrologer of their choice. We all have a stake in their survival.

Similarly, the interaction between journalist and expert will never be a simple one.

We need to see these conflicts clearly. It is conventional to speak apocalyptically about the dangers to democracy should the press decline. Yet, there is growing cynicism about the press and increasing legislative attack. One reason may be that freedom-of-the-press and the First Amendment have been invoked so often for strictly business reasons unaccompanied by inspiring editorial performance.

American democracy is peculiarly vulnerable to a loss of a serious local press. We govern a great deal in our own communities, like the schooling of our children, and we lose control as we lose knowledge.

When we were once mostly in small towns like Emporia we did most of our business face-to-face. If the local school wasn't satisfactory, we walked down and talked to the woman who ran it. If the street was full of potholes, we ran into the county commissioner at the store and told him about our ruined wheel. If the air was dirty, we asked the neighbor next door why he burned leaves on washday.

In large cities, our jobs, our education, our housing, our transportation, and the air we breathe are governed, if they are governed at all, by distant administrators whom we don't know and who don't know us. Each of these administrators arranges a tiny fraction of the lives of hundreds of thousands of people, and almost none of these administrators know the other administrators who arrange the other fractions of our lives.

Under these conditions, even the most skilled and articulate citizen has trouble controlling his environment. It is hard because the bureaucracies in our lives—in government, business, and academic life—have become massive and complicated, and consequently they are slower and less sensitive to the individual. We see one result in our universities, where many of our children find world conditions unsatisfactory and are articulate enough to make their complaints heard. But we see it most urgently in the ghetto, where conditions are intolerable and the level of bureaucratic skills the lowest.

The rebellions are not confined to the United States. Everywhere people are getting some insight through modern communications about how other people live and are comparing it with how they live. The first mass communications generation also rebels in Berlin, Russia, Ghana, Spain, and Mexico.

It is no accident that everywhere the target of the rebellion is "the system," and that there seems to be no particular common ideology. Our authorities suspect Communist influence; in Communist countries they call it capitalistic liberal intellectualism. It has more to do with the individual's perception of himself than it does with politics.

"The system" so often attacked is not usually wicked. It is usually sluggish. It has to serve too many people in too many ways, and the servers and the servees have trouble talking to each other. A successful system ought to do two things, whether it is a government, business firm, or a university: It ought to know what its people need and want, and if they are not getting what they need and want, the system ought to have a quick way to detect it.

People's needs have to be seen clearly because we live with such large systems that bad designs produce terribly large mistakes. And if a working system begins to break down somewhere, the system must find out quickly because it deals with so many people that a malfunction can cause human grief at a rapid rate.

The press has an obvious role in such a system. It is a natural vehicle for the expression of local needs. And it is a natural instrument for the detection of breakdowns in the social system. On the whole, the press has not been doing either of these tasks very well.

For one thing, too many news organizations see their job as doing no more than transmitting information that comes most easily over the transom. Few have the competence to understand the systems of government and business they should monitor. And lastly, too many are so close to officialdom that they are defensive about its performance. News organizations too devoted to the status quo resist evidence that the status quo isn't working. For too many news operations in too many communities the official, bureaucratic view of the world is the press view of the world.

It is an extension of what William Allen White called the press's weakness for "the country club complex." It is a rejection of the best journalism this country has produced. And of the best that it produces today.

All serious people in the news business have read about the dramatic rise of the pioneers in popular journalism, Hearst, Pulitzer, and E. W. Scripps. What most of us have forgotten is that they were persistent and enterprising protectors of the ordinary man against the status quo, against insensitive governments, utilities, and corporations.

Today the news corporations are eminently respectable. The thousands of journalistic outlets served by the corporate descendants of Hearst, Pulitzer, and Scripps would never run the stories and editorials their founders ran; some because they were not good stories and editorials, but also because they would be too radical and would sound too hostile to corporate leadership.

The postwar news corporations became overly establishmentarian not just from their own prosperity and stability, but because they also reflected most of us. In the postwar world our incomes began the great average rise. We lost the reformist zeal that ran through our earlier history. If I criticize journalistic organizations for becoming too fat and happy, I must add that most of us, readers and writers, also were too fat and happy. And with terrible consequences:

Our cities became crowded, noisy, and dirty even for our most affluent citizens; miserable refugees from automation and racial oppression in the rural areas piled into the centers of cities being abandoned by the newly affluent working class looking for escape in the suburbs; slum schools became machines for destroying young personalities at a frightening rate; the rebels and rejects of these schools have been living off the streets for years untouched by any imagination in schooling designed for their needs or by their own elders begging them not to destroy their ghettos, and untouched even by the bitter revolutionaries who urged them to stop burning and start shooting; and the welfare system became increasingly morbid and destructive.

These social ills were not suddenly created this year. They began to be noticeable to those looking for them in the early post-war years. Yet to this day there are millions of Americans who don't believe that these conditions have been with us all this time.

We all were insensitive to this, geographically removed because we live in one-class neighborhoods away from the unpleasantness. The average government and business bureaucrat was similarly separated from it: The people he depended on were not suffering so much. The press was not different from government or business. And that's the point: It should have been. It should be now. If local and national governments are insensitive to breakdowns in their programs, if private business is not providing for what government should not do, the newspaper and broadcasting news organizations must have the motivation and the competence to make independent judgments.

The National Advisory Commission on Civil Disorder recommended that news organizations create their own Institute of Urban Communications to train journalists to understand the problems of the city, especially the ghetto. The aim is a good one. We need to know more about urban life. But I'm not sure that such an institute is best formed by the news corporations. It would be too easy to become a narrow trade school. There are too few competent scholars in urban affairs already, and this would dissipate them. Using urban study centers in existing universities would be faster and produce more sophisticated training than a separate institute.

The present crisis in our cities should remind the news media that their environment has changed and with these changes come new obligations and, possibly, new journalistic forms.

One background reason our ghettos went unnoticed for so long is that we have lost our two most powerful institutions for democratizing and integrating Americans. One was the small community and the other was the public school in a small community.

In the separate small community, where not so long ago most Americans lived, there were within easy sight of everyone people of different ages, incomes, education, and ethnic background. Contact was constant and normal. Contact sometimes brought conflict, but it was personal, and even in conflict there was a sense of flesh-and-blood presence that made us realize that we would all have to live together.

Today we tend to live in one-class neighborhoods and communities, where most people are of the same age, income, education, type of occupation, and race. There are millions of American children who have no daily experience with old people, poor people, black people, or anyone who isn't pretty much like themselves.

In the community school children used to meet each other before adult stereotypes had fixed their image of people from different backgrounds. Today, the usual public school consists mostly of children from the same background and the same race.

These older democratizing institutions are passing, the ones that taught Americans of different kinds a doctrine of peaceful coexistence. What remains to give us as a nation a common view of each other? The mass media: Our newspapers, television and radio, and magazines. Only lately have our mass media begun to be conscious of what they tell us about each other.

Aside from this consciousness, the new obligation on the press to become intelligent detectors of malfunctions in the school system may require new forms. The news ought to do what it always was supposed to do, to inform the public of reality, no matter how unpleasant that reality might be. For events that become dramatically visible, the news media do well.

The news also needs to continue to carry the voices stimulated by public events, even voices we dislike, saying things we abhor.

The news must look always for causes of public episodes, and this should be done with competence and speed. New competence is needed because the elements of the news are more complicated than they used to be. Papers a generation ago had a large quotient of simple natural disasters and individual crime. Today they have more politics and complex social developments, all requiring a higher order of reportorial skill. This skill has to be applied quickly while the citizen is watching and is interested. When the surface events disappear, public interest tends to disappear. This is sometimes attributed to public stupidity, but it is more likely the only way all of us can remain sane in a world full of new events.

News organizations need to make their own recommendations, in editorials, also at a time when people are paying attention.

Lastly, we may need a new form in American journalism: The regular presentation of proposed solutions to leading problems by thoughtful men outside of journalism. These suggestions now appear in print in passing fragments, or in politicians' speeches, or in learned journals, and are picked up in editorials if they happen to agree with the publisher's views. But it is increasingly clear that in the rapid succession of large-scale problems of modern urban society, no single source knows enough or is wise enough to have an instant answer, not even journalists. Once a social problem has reached crisis proportions, we begin to discover that thoughtful men had earlier figured out some answers. These men are often at universities, sometimes in government, sometimes in business; sometimes they are specialists in journalism. They are the men who have spent their lives studying a problem that suddenly surfaces into public consciousness. Yet, at that moment of publicity, there is often a flood of platitudinous editorials in the news media, ignorant of the informed solutions available. I can only despair at how many good pine trees were cut down to make how many tons of newsprint to carry how many editorials damning the public welfare system over the last thirty years, while for many years there have been plausible and humane substitutes worked out by economists and social scientists. One such substitute, the negative income tax, became a respectable candidate for public consideration not through editorials but because it was recommended by the president of the Ford Motor Company.

We need a systematic collection of expert presentations of solutions to leading problems, expressed clearly and fairly. There should be a variety of these, attempting to cover the whole spectrum of ideas whether or not these ideas agree with the opinions of the news proprietor or with his professionals. This requires journalists who are in constant touch with the world of scholarship and of social action. It requires proprietors who permit presentation of these ideas based on professional and not partisan judgment. It could be the greatest contribution the news media of this country could make to the reservoir of ideas from which public understanding and public policy can find solutions to problems.

Providing a systematic review of expert solutions would help remove the stigma of monopoly opinion in the press, or of the distressing obligation for every media proprietor to pretend that he has an instant remedy for every ailment of society.

Today the news institutions of this country are increasingly competent to report the physical evidence of urgent problems. They are improving in their ability to point to causes of these problems. But in doing this they may have completed only half the necessary job. That half-job could produce unhappy consequences. In effect, the news has told every American that his life is never again going to be the same, that everyone must move. But the news media have not gone on to produce systematic information on how to move and what directions are available. This is a formula for public frustration and panic. The public needs to be informed what rational alternatives it has for action. To do this, the news media need not play God. They can play the only slightly more modest role of dean of the faculty. By regularly marshaling in clear form the ideas of others, the news media can not only alert the public to changes in its environment but add the crucial knowledge of civilized and realistic ways of coping with change.

Bill D. Moyers
The Press and Government:
Who's Telling the Truth?

Having gone over to the enemy, I have been encouraged to discuss the relationship between government and the press as I now see it. If I were to defend the administration and my work at the White House, I would be in the position of the foreman of the jury charged by the judge to bring in a not-guilty verdict in the case of a young man arrested for the theft of an automobile. "Your honor," the foreman announced dutifully, "we find the boy who stole that car not guilty."

In candor (a new word in my vocabulary since I left the White House) I must confess to an ambivalence about both the press and the government similar to the dilemma of the suitor who loves two women and is hesitant to choose between them. This is no slightly frustrating love affair; if you think it impossible to serve two masters, you should try to serve two mistresses. Nonetheless, I know of no two callings more concerned with the public interest or more satisfying to a man's sense of duty than journalism and government. If I were not in the one, I would have to be in the other.

I admit this bias because you should know that what I say about the press and government is colored by the fact that I am a creature of both. I criticize them with affection, having learned enough about the vices and virtues of these two institutions to know that neither is totally innocent nor totally guilty of all the charges they heap upon one another. I have not learned enough about them to propose solutions to all the questions each asks about the other, although my obligation to each, and their great power in a free society, compel us all constantly to ponder, question, and probe whether they are performing well.

I do know that credibility is not the government's problem alone. Public officials are not the only victims of fallibility; they are not the only human beings who see things through their own special lens. We in the press also suffer from the appearance of contradiction, which is the essence of a credibility gap.

Examples abound, but let me mention three from my own experience at the White House.

When Edwin O. Reischauer resigned as United States Ambassador to Japan, he was interviewed by the press in Tokyo. The headline in the Washington *Post* the next day read: REISCHAUER BACKS U.S. VIET POLICY. The headline in the New York

Times read: REISCHAUER CRITICAL OF VIETNAM POLICY. After a debate in the House of Commons on British support of United States policy in Vietnam, the headline in the Washington *Post* read: WILSON GETS SUPPORT FOR U.S. STAND. The headline in the New York *Times* read: COMMONS RESTRICTS BACKING ON VIETNAM. Perhaps both were correct, but was one more correct? You might be able to reconcile the difference if you could read the full report in both papers, but for most people that is not an option. They do not have the opportunity to weigh the differences between contradictory stories.

Again. The day before the elections in South Vietnam in 1965, one commentator for the Columbia Broadcasting System declared: "The armed forces have been turned loose in the get-out-the-vote movement. In the South Vietnamese army, like any other, an order is an order. But if the voters have to be driven to the polls with guns and bayonets, so to speak, it would appear that the Viet Cong has made its point about the Ky regime's popular support." The day after the election, however, another CBS commentator expressed amazement that so many South Vietnamese turned out to vote against the Viet Cong. "After all," he said, "the government of South Vietnam is not driving the people to the polls with bayonets." If you had heard both reports, you might have asked: "What's going on here? Was one of the reporters not telling the truth? Was one right and the other wrong?" The answer is probably that each man was partially wrong and partially right, because each man saw what *he* was looking at, or looking for. "Who's telling the truth?" a correspondent friend of mine was asked when he returned from Vietnam. "Nearly everybody," he answered. "Nearly everybody out there bears true witness to his bias and his senses."

The nuances in these and other examples bear that out, and the point remains: The appearance of contradiction is a problem for the press, too. Like government officials, journalists look at ideas and events through their own eyes. There is nothing wrong with that practice: The mistake is to pass it off as something other than the pursuit of truth by men less opinionated than their peers.

I learned at the White House that of all the great myths of American journalism, objectivity is the greatest. Each of us sees what his own experience leads him to see. What is happening often depends upon who is looking. Depending on who is looking and writing, the White House is brisk or brusque, assured or arrogant, casual or sloppy, frank or brutal, warm or corny, cautious or timid, compassionate or condescending, reserved or callous. As press secretary, I resented this. As a publisher, I guess I must accept it.

Does the press really permit its humanity to interfere in the search for truth? I submit the evidence of Richard Harwood, then of the Louisville *Courier-Journal,* now of the Washington *Post,* who reported not too long after President Johnson was in office that several long-time correspondents at the White House, when asked why the President's honeymoon with the press had ended, gave this answer: "Although Johnson has made even more of an effort than Kennedy to cultivate and woo the press, most White House reporters don't care for him as a person. They liked Kennedy and enjoyed his company. Johnson hasn't won their affection." My irascible friend Ted Lewis, of the New York *Daily News,* asked: "What sort of journalism is that? It suggests that unless the President wins the 'affection' of the White House press, he is not going to get fair treatment." You may be right, Ted, although I rarely encountered reporters who were intentionally unfair to the President because he had failed to win their affection. No one begrudges a reporter his feelings, only the righteous indignation he expresses when it is suggested that he is an error-prone human being first and a journalist second.

All of this is so obvious that the question arises, "Why discuss it?" The first part of the answer has to do with the professional longevity of the journalist. For all practical purposes we are beyond retaliation. We almost always have the last word because we are simply more durable. While the public can turn out officials whose integrity is exposed as unethical or whose judgments are consistently wrong or whose talents are proven to be inadequate, journalists do not operate at the end of an electorate's whim. The press can claim with Lord Tennyson's brook:

> I chatter, chatter, as I flow
> To join the brimming river,
> For men may come and men may go,
> But I go on for ever.

There is an even more important reason for examining our vision. It has to do with the crisis of confidence in America today. Many of our colleagues believe the crisis affects public officials only. They are wrong. In the last year I have spoken at colleges and universities in every part of the country, to be confronted on each campus with a biting doubt about the veracity of both government and the press. One student in the Midwest said: "You know, Mr. Moyers, you have served in government and journalism, so it is doubly hard to believe anything you say." That remark says a great deal about the state of America today, and the state of America is disturbing. We seem on the way to becoming a nation of cynics. While skepticism is the mark of a healthy climate in a democracy, cynicism—widespread cynicism directed at the basic institutions of a society—can cripple a nation's will and undermine her spirit. A cynic, Lord Darlington told Cecil Graham, is a man who knows the price of everything and the value of nothing. And that is true of a cynical nation.

Cynicism about the press and government ultimately will infect the very core of the way we transact our public affairs; it will eat at the general confidence we must be able to have in one another if a pluralistic society is to work.

"The fundamental issue is the question of trust," James Reston has written. "The most serious problem in America today is that there is widespread doubt in the public mind about its major leaders and institutions. There is more troubled questioning of the veracity of statements out of the White House today than at any time in recent memory. The cynicism about the Congress is palpable. The disbelief in the press is a national joke . . . . There is little public trust today." And only recently, David Broder, one of the most perceptive of the young political reporters in Washington, reported spending a weekend in Pennsylvania, away from the political wars, only to find his hosts wanting to know if they can "truly trust anything the politicians, the press, or the public officials—the principal agents in the political process—say or write."

I have heard some of my colleagues in journalism say: "Well, you have a point, but most government officials lie deliberately, 'in the name of national security,' while our mistakes are not intended." The reply is that we can lose our credibility in the fashion many ladies lose their virtue—with the very best of intentions.

Many young people constantly point to examples of innocent discrepancy in expressing doubts about what they read. Take, as one example, the coverage last year of the protest in the United Nations Building plaza. One headline read: 100,000 RALLY AT UN AGAINST WAR. Another account reported flatly that at least 300,000 had marched. One student told me, "We might forgive journalists for not being able to write, but how can we forgive you for not admitting that you can't count?" Every political reporter knows how difficult it is to assess the size of a crowd, and no one has yet to offer a sure way of improving our estimates. The fact remains that people are not willing to recognize such handicaps in judging whether we are to be believed or not. Virtue, I repeat, can be lost quite innocently.

As citizens, you and I should be worried when millions of people believe the government lies. As journalists, we should be equally concerned when millions of people believe the press lies, too. We would all no doubt be amazed at the number of people, especially the young, who agree with the assertion, "An ambassador is a man of virtue sent to lie abroad for his country, and a journalist is a man without virtue who lies at home for himself." If you think this an exaggerated view of how we are regarded, pause long enough to recall the scene at the Republican convention in San Francisco in 1964 as thousands of delegates stood and shook their fists at the press bleachers when President Eisenhower denounced those "sensation-seeking columnists and commentators." A reporter who was there admitted to me that he feared more for his safety at that moment than he did in the riot-engulfed streets of Detroit three years later.

If there are growing numbers of people willing to believe the worst about the press, they are supported by quite sincere men in public life ready to convince them that their worst fears are justified. Who was responsible for the plunging fortunes of George Romney last winter? Not George Romney, but the press! "One of the most unfair things that has happened in the last two and a half years," he said, "was the effort by the press to create the idea that I have been inconsistent and wobbly and didn't understand the situation."

And why do public doubts exist about the Vietnam war? Not because of the tenacity of the Viet Cong, the complexities of a brutish war, nor the natural revulsion to the horrors of war. No;

to hear military officials tell it, these public doubts can be traced to a "cynical element" of the press in Saigon.

There are always people eager to prove that the press is responsible for their misfortune; the more they succeed in casting doubts on the veracity of the press, the more we have to work to clean our own house.

What specifically can we do? There is no overall cure. The suggestions I make are obvious and familiar. They simply need to be stated again and again as part of the vigilance that is the price of the power and obligation of the press.

First, we should act with the same appreciation of candor about ourselves that we expect of public officials. This would lead to several improvements: An admission of the subjectivity of our objectivity; a confession that not even the press can discover the "whole truth and nothing but the truth"—that at best we can only come up with the "bits and pieces of truth"; and an acknowledgment that our responsibility is greater than the skill with which we pretend to discharge it.

Second, we should either be prepared to live apart from tangling alliances with officialdom or be prepared to give up the illusion that we do. There is considerable public skepticism about the cozy ties between the press and governments at every level, and much of this skepticism is justified. In Washington, I discovered, the temptation is often for both government and the press to think of themselves as brokers of the public interest rather than its guardians; the line between the parallel but competing objectives of the two tends to be blurred as officials and journalists "join the Establishment." As Stewart Alsop says in his new book on Washington, "Information is to any journalist what water is to a perpetually thirsty man, and when a politician or official is a supplier of information as well as a friend, it is impossible to be objective." Alsop, an enterprising and respected reporter, reveals just how impossible when he admits that he and Charles Bartlett submitted their now-famous *Saturday Evening Post* article on the Cuban missile crisis to President Kennedy, who read it "for accuracy." Kennedy suggested that the authors eliminate the name of one adviser from their list of "doves" because of the fear that Congress would reopen an attack on the man's wartime record as a pacifist. The authors obliged the President, feeling, I am sure, that they were being humane to do so. Well they may have been, too, because both are honest and thoughtful; but they were also doing a favor for a politician.

I sought on several occasions to get a reporter to let me check his copy "for accuracy." I succeeded only twice, which record attests to the unwillingness of many journalists to play it too cozy. When they fail to resist, whatever the motive, they risk the confidence of the public. The press may be sure of its integrity, but the issue is how we look to others—to our readers in particular. Unless we see ourselves as Caesar's wife we are likely to be seen as Antony's Cleopatra.

The third suggestion for improving our credibility is just as fundamental as a freshman journalism course—and like those courses, as taken for granted. It is to make accuracy again the first rule of reporting. I hesitate among such veterans and experts to make the point, but nothing undermines the credibility of the press like sloppy reporting.

I know something about this from first-hand experience. I made a speech in Alabama which was begun by an attempt to be humorous. There were, I said, some very pleasant experiences at the White House, and some not so pleasant. For example, I cited a heated exchange with Walter Cronkite. The President heard about it and called me and said, "Bill, did you call Walter Cronkite a liar?" "Yes, sir, I did." "And did you call him irresponsible and ignorant?" "Yes, sir, I did." "And did you also say he was a biased and arrogant stooge for CBS?" "No, Mr. President, I forgot that!" As the audience stopped laughing, I said: "So you can see that I didn't always enjoy being White House press secretary."

I went on to tell the audience: All of you have heard of planted questions—where the press secretary suggests to reporters questions they should ask because the President has something on a subject he wants to be sure to say. Well, I said, "That is not a new practice; every press secretary has engaged in it for very good reasons. But I was the first press secretary to move on to planted questions; we gave the answer and let the reporter guess the question."

What was carried of those remarks in one of the large Alabama dailies and picked up by one of the wire services? A brief story reporting soberly: "As for his post at the White House, Mr. Moyers said: 'I never enjoyed being press secretary.' A part of his job was to plant questions for reporters to ask the President be-cause those were the questions the President was prepared to answer." The implication was that I did not like being press secretary because I had to plant questions. I have yet to live that report down. Only a few days ago the editor of a national maga-zine saw it and asked me to write a 1,500-word piece on why I quit the White House in protest of such shady practices as planting questions!

I tell this story merely to illustrate the larger point—that bad reporting creates unbelievers. When people read an inaccurate account of their own activities, they will tend to doubt everything else they read, too. It is a sad reflection on the state of our repu-tation today that far more readers believe the advice they get from Ann Landers than they do the advice of our editorials.

My fourth suggestion goes to the heart of one of the most common but dangerous practices in Washington today, one that constantly afflicts the credibility of the press and government—the indiscriminate use of backgrounders as the source of "hard" news stories. I propose that members of the Washington press adopt some basic ground rules for backgrounders and seek to get govern-ment officials to recognize and respect those rules.

The backgrounder is an old Washington institution. It is more endured than revered. The original purpose was to permit a government official to talk freely to newsmen without worry that some offhand remark would embarrass him, his agency, or the government. For that purpose it still has merit. But as Allen Otten of the *Wall Street Journal,* among others, has recently pointed out, "The anonymity of the backgrounder has been in-creasingly abused to test public reaction to new schemes and pro-jected appointments, to mobilize opinion behind government projects, and to advance one agency's cause or one politician's cause against others."

Individual reporters, as Otten emphasized, constantly seek in-formation on a "background" basis from officials. They want as complete a story as possible, and frequently, in order to receive particular pieces of a story, have to promise not to quote the man they are talking to or even his agency. But the individual reporter seeking background information on his own has a full opportu-nity to cross-examine his witness, to check the evidence with other sources later, to choose information he regards reliable and accurate, and to throw away the self-serving propaganda.

Formal group briefings, however, are quite another matter. They tend often to degenerate into a relationship between the public official and reporters not unlike that of amanuensis to master. The competitive pressure permits little time for cross-checking and contributes to uniformity—as if the press corps were a delayed-action Greek chorus—and that, indeed, is what the public officials want. Their objective is to get out what the government wants to get out, as the government wants it to get out—a quite natural and understandable ambition.

The dangers in this practice should be clear to anyone. For one thing, anonymity is fearless, and if a public official wants to do so, and can find a journalist willing to cooperate, he can hide behind that anonymity to grind an axe or float a balloon, all the while protecting himself from possible adverse reaction by fuzzing the source. Does this happen often? Well, my former colleague, Arthur Sylvester, who is a fairly blunt man, recently admitted quite bluntly that for six years, while he served as the Pentagon's chief information officer, he watched cover-up stories go down smooth as cream when he thought they would cause a frightful gurgle.

Another danger is public confusion. I was once in a television control room at a moment when we could not see who was speaking although we could hear at least a dozen voices from the studio. I thought at the time how bewildered newspaper readers must be when they read information from a plethora of unidentified sources. How can we expect people to judge the reliability of a statement if it is attributed only to an "informed source"?

How do you expect your readers really to know if Governor Rockefeller has or has not changed his position on Vietnam if you read that "sources close to the Governor" hint that he has one day, and that he hasn't the next? And how do you know if John Lindsay believes Charles Percy is a better man for President than Nelson Rockefeller if the stories from Washington say he does and the stories from New York City a few days later say he doesn't? Suppose, just to make a point, that instead of James Reston's by-line on his column, there appeared only these words: "By a high official of the New York *Times*." And in the place of the name of Tom Wicker there appeared only: "By a reliable source." They would be just as readable, but would they carry that urgent reliability essential to public trust in public information?

The issue becomes more critical, of course, when the people's understanding of public policy is clouded because certain information is deliberately divorced from its source.

In August, 1966, an official in Saigon gave a backgrounder in which he made statements that led reporters to believe that studies made in the Pentagon forecast a long war in Vietnam, a war perhaps of eight years. Another study, it was said, estimated it would take 750,000 United States troops in Vietnam to end the war in five years (at the time we had 290,000 men there). The President then told a news conference that Secretary McNamara could find no evidence of any such studies having been made in Defense. McNamara, the President added, said he did not agree with the estimates. Later, sources identified only as "U.S. officials" —again on a background basis—said no such studies had been made, except perhaps as one man's opinion, and that estimates of the length of the war were worthless anyway. The source of the original backgrounder turned out to be Marine Corps Commandant General Wallace M. Greene, but whom was the public to believe: the "high official" in Saigon or the "U.S. officials" in Washington?

There are other, even more incongruous, examples. Samuel J. Archibald, formerly head of the staff of the Foreign Operations and Government Information Subcommittee, tells of an episode in his lucid story of government backgrounders in the Winter issue of the *Columbia Journalism Review*. "Secretary of State Dulles," he wrote, "was the anonymous source for a story in 1953 that his department was considering a Korean boundary settlement along the line of the narrow waist of the Korean peninsula. The trial balloon was shot down on Capitol Hill. So another anonymous source came out of the White House denying there was any consideration of a permanent division of Korea. This White House statement also was drafted by Dulles. The government ghost had denied his own previous story."

More recently—in November of 1967—General Westmoreland told a group of reporters in Washington that he was "deeply concerned" that the Cambodian port of Sihanoukville was about to become an important source of arms for Viet Cong troops in

South Vietnam. The military, he added, was considering contingency plans to quarantine the port. The reporters present agreed to hold their stories, quoting "some U.S. officials," until the general had left town. The aim of the exercise, reporters later reasoned, was to put extra heat on Cambodian Premier Sihanouk to crack down on the arms shipments and to spur international action toward the same end. A worthwhile objective, no doubt; but was it necessary for several reporters to deceive the public into thinking that "some U.S. officials" rather than one in particular was considering such a significant shift of policy? Did it not occur to the reporters that the United States government has more effective and legitimate ways to get a message of such import to Prince Sihanouk and to spur international action than to compromise the boundary between an independent press and a government which always seeks to make that press an ally in furthering its policies? Is the press justified in condemning "deception and concealment" by government officials if the press, however good its intentions, is itself a party to deception and concealment?

The practice is not at all confined to the government, of course. If you will permit another personal testimony: I was awakened about midnight one night with a call from a wire service reporter in Washington saying that his agency was moving a story out of St. Louis quoting "top sources" of the National Council of Churches. They alleged that a policy statement which would have sharply criticized administration policy in Vietnam had been watered down after phone calls from me. The council sources gave the information on the condition that their names be withheld. They said the calls were an attempt to stop outright endorsement of a World Council of Churches resolution.

There was absolutely no truth to the charges. I was not even aware that the Council of Churches was meeting in St. Louis. I had had no contact with anyone at the council on the question of any resolution concerning Vietnam. I denied the charges, of course, and my denial finally made the second paragraph of a later story. At first I was angry that such a charge would be moved before it was checked with the accused. Then I was disturbed because a major news organization could be used to provide a platform for anonymous accusations against public officials or private citizens.

It occurred to me that someone should have had the guts to say to those sources, even if they were church officials: "Sure, we'll run your accusation—if you will stand behind it in print or if you will tell us to whom and at what time the calls were made."

I had cooled down considerably the next morning, and drove to work amused by the thought of ministers employing techniques government officials and politicians had found so effective in dealing with adversaries. If clergymen had only learned these techniques earlier, I decided, that marvelous thirteenth chapter of I. Corinthians might read: "Though I speak with the tongues of men and of angels, and have not love, I am become as sounding brass, or a tinkling cymbal, a source close to St. Paul said today."

All of this may strike you as somewhat hypocritical, coming as it does from someone who made his living by backgrounding the press. But I was troubled by the process, as were many of the reporters with whom I dealt, because while we knew the careful backgrounder to be useful and necessary, especially in the area of national security, we also felt it had become a habit of convenience, a rule rather than an exception. There was no question but that opinions and predictions, indictments and speculation, coming from a host of anonymous spokesmen were only increasing the public's apprehension about the credibility of what it reads and what it is told.

Can restraint be brought to the use of backgrounders in Washington? Previous efforts of reform have been shortlived, but because public confidence is at stake, I am convinced new efforts should be made. It is naïve to believe that the practice will be abandoned altogether, or even should be. As Jules Frandsen, veteran head of the Washington bureau of United Press International, has said: "A lot of skulduggery in government and in Congress would never come to light if everything had to be attributed. Employees often can't afford to risk their jobs by talking for attribution." Nonetheless, the practice is so consistently abused that some commonly accepted ground rules are in order.

A step in the right direction would be for representatives of the various press organizations to meet and try to agree among themselves on these ground rules. They could then request a meeting with the President-elect after the elections to seek his support in getting the new administration to recognize and respect the rules.

Having tried on several occasions to mediate between journalists and the government, I am not sanguine about the possibility of reaching agreement within or among either group on what the ground rules for backgrounders should be. As a point of departure for trying, here are eight principles which I believe would help to bring some order into a ritual that at the moment can only be as confusing to the public as Haitian voodoo.

1: Backgrounders should be designed to explain policy rather than announce policy. This rule would discourage the use of unattributed quotations which turn "soft news" into "hard news."

2: Backgrounders in subjects other than national security and foreign affairs should be the exception rather than the rule.

3: The contents of a group backgrounder should not be disclosed for at least one hour after the conclusion of the session. This would permit time for cross-checking. It would also reduce the possibility of a public official using a backgrounder strictly for self-serving purposes. To quote Allen Otten again, "It may be necessary to report that the government is viewing a particular event as a great victory, but the reporter who has good reason to believe the government isn't certainly seems obliged to insert pertinent information to suggest the official view may be somewhat colored." To do this, the reporter needs time.

4: The rules should be clearly stated, before the backgrounder begins, by the principal or by his press spokesman.

5: There should be only two levels of concealment. Either the reporter uses the information on his own—a practice that should be reserved for the most sensitive issues of national security—or it should be attributed as stated in the following principle.

6: The source should be identified by his specific agency. The loose anonymity of "high U.S. official," "top government officials," "friends of the President," or "visitors who've talked to the President" would be replaced by "a Defense Department spokesman" or "a U.S. Army official" or "White House sources." The reader would still be in doubt as to the authenticity and the reliability of the information, but the burden of proof would not be altogether on the press.

7: The reporters should refuse to deliberately increase the obfuscation through such tactics as withholding the information until the source has left town or by attributing the information to plural sources when it comes in fact from one source.

8: When a public official in a backgrounder refuses to permit attribution of material that is patently self-serving but reporters nonetheless feel obliged to carry the story, they should carry a sentence attributing the information to a Pentagon (or State or White House) official "whose name is withheld at his insistence."

I offer these suggestions only as the starting point for serious discussions by journalists and public officials. Other men will have better proposals. The important task is for the press to make some effort to deal with the problem. I am aware that a backgrounder is useful to a public official and to a reporter, helping the one to get his viewpoint across and the other to gain valuable insight or information that he could not get if the official were required to speak for attribution. But I also know that what is convenient to the government and to the press is confusing to the public. These ideas are put forward with the *public* in mind. As far as the relationship between the press and the government is concerned, these suggestions tip the scale in favor of the press. That is deliberate. Most reporters in Washington go along with the existing arrangements for backgrounders because they feel they must—"that's the name of the game." They do so knowing that in most cases they are serving the government's interest more than their own. I am confident most reporters want and would welcome some attempt to agree on ground rules that would make it less necessary for them to compromise the appearance of integrity and independence.

Whatever rules are agreed upon, the problem will be in getting the government to respect them. But even that is not so formidable an obstacle as it appears. Government officials only call a backgrounder to brief a large press gathering when those officials have something to put out. If the newspapers and the media most read and watched by Washington officials—in particular, the three networks, the wire services, and the Washington and New York City press—insist that the rules by which they will transmit the information be followed, respect for rules will grow in time. And with it the credibility of the American press.

Now we come to the credibility of the Government. We have arrived at "Credibility Gap."

Time and time again I am asked: Do Presidents really lie? And press secretaries? I reply: Before there were Presidents and press secretaries, there were Adam and Eve, and there is a little of each of them in all of us.

The question, however, goes far beyond a simple affirmation

that public officials are human. The press has an obligation to increase the public's understanding of the credibility gap since we have certainly increased the public's awareness of it. I have no question but that we in the government overreacted to the charges of incredibility, partly because any man smarts and grows defensive when his integrity is assaulted. But if we have overreacted, the press has underexplained. The credibility gap became an overworked catch phrase that many people took for granted because they heard it repeated so often. What was otherwise an imprecise and poorly defined term took on the familiarity of an established creed which people read without thinking and repeat without understanding.

There has always been a credibility problem; the term is no recent addition to our political nomenclature. Some people trace it back to Plato's premise that "The rulers of the State are the only ones who should have the privilege of lying, either at home or abroad; they may be allowed to lie for the good of the State." Plato has his apostles to this day; but they are not legion— they do not even often wind up in high places, fortunately. We will not be able to locate enough pathological liars in official Washington to dig a very deep credibility gap.

Nor can the problem be traced merely to the obsessive tendency of public officials to be wrong in their predictions. That is a phenomenon of human nature, whether in public office or in the press. What better proof than the headlines that have appeared over the last few months in different American newspapers: "KENNEDY WILL SUPPORT JOHNSON"; "ROMNEY IS IN IT FOR KEEPS"; "KENNEDY WILL NOT RUN"; "ROCKE-FELLER TO ENTER OREGON PRIMARY"; "JOHNSON WON'T QUIT."

No, we have to look elsewhere for a fuller understanding of the matter. I am familiar with all the charges and with the evidence: the erroneous predictions of military progress, the attempts to put the best face on every crisis, the fiscal confusion, the stories of peace feelers raised and peace feelers dashed, and so on. But it is not as simple as all that, and some things should be said to put the problem into perspective.

There were times when we were less than candid in government about important matters which were not related to national security. You should be relieved to know that we were almost always found out. The Washington press corps, by and large, is a persistent posse, and no administration will escape being called into account for its mistakes and sins. I was often angered by reporters, especially those who jumped to conclusions and those who found it forever impossible to give the government any benefit of a doubt; but secretly, if not always openly, I could not help but admire the handiwork of an enterprising reporter who probed through the smokescreens and cut into the complexities to piece a story together. Your sins will find you out—and with the help of a good reporter, they will find you out all the sooner.

But the problem of credibility is far more complicated. For the purpose of perspective rather than exoneration, I would like to make a few observations about some of the factors that make this a difficult issue.

First, some things are simply not suited for telling on the time schedule an inquisitive press prefers. At the risk of appearing to hide the facts, a President must often remain quiet. This is especially true when a President deals with a crisis over which he has little control but for which he must assume great responsibility. The Pueblo incident comes to mind. As a journalist, I was quick to say: Tell us more. But as one who has been there, I can appreciate why silence is sometimes the wisest policy.

I am not speaking of the deep-seated propensity for clandestine conduct that led one official to put a sign on his desk which said: "The secrecy of my job does not permit me to know what I am doing." I am speaking of the necessity for a President to resist commenting on a situation until he can be certain his words will produce the intended result. President Harding learned this the hard way when he jeopardized the disarmament conference of 1921 by giving reporters an off-the-cuff interpretation of the treaty. What he did not know was that his Secretary of State had already given the press his own interpretation of the treaty—and the two were at odds.

It is an axiom of the press that we will not hesitate to hustle a President's priorities if we can; we forget that diplomacy and political maneuvers, like film, can curl up and die from exposure. Nuclear overkill is a daily concern of a President; verbal overkill ought to be, too. Reporters should do their best to find out what is going on, but they must also recognize that the President has no obligation to spoonfeed them with a full disclosure of every facet of official thinking on every subject they see fit to probe.

Observation number two: Events make lies out of the best promises. Circumstances change, and so must a President's strategy. His best intentions may be aborted as a result, and he may end up in public having said one thing and doing another. But a President may sometimes do what he wishes; most of the time he may do what is right; he must always do what is necessary, and what is necessary changes with time and events. Thomas Jefferson no doubt was sincere when he opposed the creation of a national bank before he became President. Woodrow Wilson surely meant what he said about keeping us out of war, but circumstances overtook him and he found it necessary to do what he did not intend to do. In 1964, Lyndon Johnson declared that he sought no wider war in Southeast Asia, that he would not send American boys to do the fighting for Asian boys. One year later he widened the war and American boys were sent to fight it. For these decisions the President has been accused of breaking faith with the American people, of lying, of deliberately doing what he had said he would not do, of creating the credibility gap. It if were only that simple! Even when it leads him to be at odds with his former position, a President can ill afford to have a closed mind or to fail to do what *he* believes is best, no matter what he said or believed earlier.

A third observation: a President must sometimes reach conclusions from inconclusive evidence. There are times when a decision seems imperative before all the evidence is in. The choice may be between acting on the basis of information at hand—inconclusive though it be—or not to act at all. But Presidents know that each decision—to act or not to act—can have far-reaching consequences. No one could prove that the Marines were needed to save the lives of Americans at the Embajador Hotel in Santo Domingo, but his ambassador was telling the President that those lives were endangered. Later the press and others, with the benediction of hindsight, would argue that they were not required. The President, at the moment of decision, was not conducting a post-mortem. He was acting on the basis of immediate but inconclusive reports from the field; his decision was to commit. Only later would he be able more dispassionately to analyze more complete information.

I have made these points from the government's point of view in an effort to build at least a small bridge across the credibility gap. It is a shaky beginning at best, and I know how the view looks from the other side—the press's side—as well.

I know how incredible some of the claims of government are. I used to make them—although I was gone last year when the Department of Transportation revealed how the Bureau of Public Roads was bringing God back to American life. One of the department's press releases began:

"There are 36 churches located alongside the 60-mile Interstate Beltway (I-495) which rings the Nation's capital. And half of them have been built since 1958 when the route of the circumferential highway first became known. This, according to spokesmen of the Department of Transportation's Federal Highway Administration, points up vividly the importance of the highway transportation system to the country's community life."

This is known as straining the obvious.

A more serious cause of incredibility has been raised by Ted Lewis of the New York *Daily News*. Last year he wrote a column in which he quoted the statement made in 1963 by Secretary of Defense Robert McNamara that American troops could begin to be withdrawn from South Vietnam by 1965. Lewis was reprimanded by a spokesman for the Pentagon for writing that there had definitely been a "deliberate effort by Defense Secretary McNamara . . . to make things look better than they were." In quoting from the White House statement of October 2, 1963, he was told, "You have overlooked the very important final paragraph of that statement. It reads: 'The political situation in South Vietnam remains deeply serious. The United States had made clear its continuing opposition to any repressive action in South Vietnam. While such actions have not yet significantly affected the military effort, they could do so in the future.' "

Lewis did not bother to reply to the spokesman, even though, at Hickam Air Force Base, six weeks after the issuance of the statement in December, Secretary McNamara had again talked about some United States personnel being able to "return by the end of this year."

Why did the newspapers at the time latch on to prediction about troop returns? Lewis asked. "Because people wanted to know how long our boys would be over there."

"My point is," he wrote me, "that there is a natural oversimplification in news handling due to limited space and public interest. Responsible government officials should know this. If a statement is distorted out of context, it is because it was susceptible to an honest oversimplification. Why don't people in Washington realize this is the heart of the credibility problem? McNamara's own case is only one of hundreds. He promised—in effect—when he should have expressed hope it would turn out that way."

Secretary McNamara unquestionably meant well. But Ted Lewis has a point. Many good intentions have gone awry in Washington, and the confidence of Americans in the veracity of the government has diminished.

It is not possible to restore overnight what has been lost over the years, but a few steps can be taken at the top that will establish a climate of candor which is necessary for building trust between government, press, and people. If the new President wishes to work in such an environment, he should begin with four simple but essential elements:

First, regular press conferences—at least one each month—the purpose of which should not be to announce the news but to explain the news. The timing of press conferences, as I believed at the White House, must fit the convenience of the President, but they should be scheduled and they should be frequent. And, despite all of the shortcomings, they should also be televised.

Second, access for the press to second- and third-level officials in the White House and in each department—men below the President and the Cabinet secretaries who know the details of what is happening, and who can increase a reporter's understanding and knowledge without abusing his responsibility.

Third, minimum use of backgrounders and unattributed quotations. The indiscriminate practice smacks of the secretiveness that Americans resist as alien to an open society.

Fourth, a willingness to live and let live. Some Presidents have regarded the press as an instrument of government, not an independent arm of the people. Some have been eager to woo the press, others to criticize it. Some have wished to make cronies of reporters, others to make cheerleaders of them. Modern Presidents have realized that they can never effectively govern unless they learn to reach the people through the mass media, and the wise ones have discovered how to go through or over the press to the people.

What the press and government should seek from each other is a mutual no-poaching agreement.

For the press and the government are not allies. They are adversaries. That should be repeated. They are adversaries. Each has a special place in our scheme of things. The President was created by the Constitution and the press is protected by the Constitution—the one with the mandate to conduct the affairs of state, the other with the privilege of trying to find out all it can about what is going on.

How each performs is crucial to the workings of a system that is both free and open but fallible and fragile. For it is the nature of a democracy to thrive upon conflict between press and government without being consumed by it.

I have raised more questions than I can answer. But I did so because if neither the government nor the press can take for granted the confidence of the people, each of us must guard against poorly formed judgments about the other and against an unperturbable sense of security about our own well-being.

All of this is important because we are in quite difficult straits in this country. The deepest crises are not Vietnam and the cities but cynicism about the political order and a corroded confidence in our ability to communicate with one another and to trust one another. For such crises the requirements are large—to revive the public spirit, to restore political vigor, and to rouse the nation from her present querulous divisions to a new sense of purpose.

The government has quite a duty, for the issues must be made plain, the truth clear, if these things are to be done. But the role of the press is no less. As William Allen White said, "This nation will survive, this state will prosper, this orderly business of life will go forward if only men can speak in whatever way given them to utter what their hearts hold—by voice, by postal card, by letters, or by press." *Especially* by the press.

Carl T. Rowan
The Mass Media in an Era of
Explosive Social Change

It is axiomatic that we journalists flail other people so constantly we feel conscience-bound to indulge in a bit of self-flagellation whenever we assemble and talk about the role of journalism in our society.

I probably shall resort to a bit of self-criticism, but I wish to insure that you understand the premises that mitigate the vehemence of any indictment I make. I begin with the fundamental conviction that journalism is people. Thus it bears, and will forever bear, the mark of men's frailties, their selfishness, their ignorance, their prejudices. We can never hope for much more than to replace a little selfishness with some social consciousness, a bit of ignorance with some of that trifle of wisdom man manages to rescue from the deluge of time, a little prejudice with some of the understanding that comes with knowledge and wisdom.

Consider the great issues of war and peace, of life and death, of the hope clutched to the hearts of millions everywhere that mankind will not fall victim to a thermonuclear holocaust. How do we journalists deal with this hope? What we say to our readers, and how we say it, is surely conditioned by our own ideologies, our own notions about what ought to be the shape of future world society.

One publisher, or editor, or columnist, may be firmly of the view that force is the only thing really respected in this world. He believes that the exercise of greater force by the United States is all that will keep capitalism dominant in the world. So he deplores, and urges his readers to deplore, what he considers a "no win" policy in Vietnam. Anything short of all-out military assault is, for this journalist, "appeasement of godless communism."

For another journalist, war is immoral—period. Almost nothing justifies it. Certainly, as he sees it, the United States has no business trying to determine the shape of the future in distant places. Neo-isolationism he sees as the only safe, sane policy in the world.

Now we are going to confront these two journalists with a few paragraphs from a speech made by Robert McNamara before he stepped down as Secretary of Defense—three very important paragraphs:

"Technology has now circumscribed us all with a conceivable horizon of horror that could dwarf any catastrophe that has befallen man in his more than a million years on earth.

"The blunt fact is that neither the Soviet Union nor the United States can attack the other without being destroyed in retaliation. Nor can either of us attain a first-strike capability in the foreseeable future.

"While thermonuclear power is inconceivably awesome and represents virtually unlimited potential destructiveness, it has proven to be a limited diplomatic instrument. Its uniqueness lies in the fact that it is at one and the same time an all-powerful weapon and a very inadequate weapon."

As far as this journalist is concerned, McNamara set forth some facts that are basic to any consideration of this country's place in the world. I read him as saying that any step by either country that carries a clear risk of war between the United States and the Soviet Union is a step bordering on lunacy. I read him as saying that nuclear weapons have altered not only warfare, but diplomacy, because they have taken some of the credibility from the threatened use of force as a way of forcing another country to do our bidding. Witness our failure to impress the North Koreans with our show of naval force after they seized the USS Pueblo. I read McNamara as saying that, setting aside our vast nuclear arsenal which we are obviously loathe to use, the United States is not a great power in conventional military terms. I read McNamara as explaining why we have been bogged down in a nasty war half a world away—a war just big enough to divide the American people but not big enough to unite them.

I have no doubt that some of my colleagues come to some different conclusions about the meaning of a "nuclear stalemate" in world affairs. Many editors and publishers and columnists are utterly unprepared to accept a condition where we may for decades be running about in a frenzy, trying to put out the brush fires of "national liberation" inspired and abetted by the Soviet Union and/or Communist China. No matter what McNamara said, they would see wisdom in some kind of ultimatum to Russia, to China, to Cuba.

And that is only a fragment of the diversity, the contradictions, that are endemic to this business of reporting and interpreting for a great, complex society the events and acts that are of real meaning.

Indeed, as I go forward in my discourse on "The Mass Media in an Era of Explosive Social Change," I must note that we journalists operate in an era of grim contradictions.

Men yearn for peace as they yearn for nothing else, but still they fight with a savagery unexceeded at any time in human history.

Black men fight and die in disproportionate numbers in distant paddies and jungles, all in the name of freedom; but black Americans also die in the streets of South Carolina because one arrogant, stupid man wants to keep his bowling alley lily-white.

We plant a rocket on the moon with a robot ditch-digger, and seconds after we on earth order that robot to dig, it digs; still, we fathers cannot communicate with our sons, or mothers with daughters, or black Americans with white.

We enjoy an abundance never known to any society, with booze, baubles, and banquets within reach of many; yet we are told that the dollar is sick, the treasury is bare, and we can afford to pay for our foreign follies but not for the deepest human needs of thirty million Americans who still know squalor, hunger, and broad human want.

Oh, I could cite enough painful contradictions to make someone scream, "Is there a psychiatrist in the house?" But that is not my mission.

I am here to talk about the role of the mass media in erasing some of these contradictions. I am here to discuss how, through the press and the tube, we can mobilize in our generation some of the wisdom and compassion that were the mark of William Allen White. I am here to explore means through which some of us may serve as true citizens of our towns and our world and leave on them the same marks of courage and insight that William Allen White left on his town and his times.

As I see it, there are going to be two great issues in this country this year. One will be foreign policy, which is another way of saying the war in Vietnam. The other is likely to be civil rights, which some people would describe as rioting and turbulence in the great cities of America.

In each of these areas, the press is going to have a tremendous lot to do in determining whether the American press reacts with emotion, with anger, and, in some instances with stupidity. Or whether it reacts with some measure of insight, and wisdom, and compassion. How will the press respond?

It has become a commonplace for Americans—especially journalists—to deplore our communications failures. We know that the President isn't getting through to Ho Chi Minh; that Americans aren't on the same wavelength as the mainland Chinese; that black Americans aren't communicating with white Americans; that poor people of all races feel alienated from affluent Americans of all races. We deplore all this out of a suspicion that Boston might have survived an era in which the Lowells talked only to the Cabots and the Cabots talked only to God—but that neither this world nor today's cities can survive the festering animosities, the violent explosions, that erupt largely because we do not, or will not, communicate with each other.

I think I became most acutely aware of the magnitude of this problem when I was director of the United States Information Agency—and charged, of course, with the most mammoth communications assignment one could possibly be given. We were supposed to communicate to the South Vietnamese the nobleness of American intentions—and sufficient respect and understanding of the Saigon government as to provoke peasants to give the kind of loyalties to Saigon that they had never given to any central government.

We were supposed to communicate to North Vietnam the harsh reality of American resolution; but at the same time the tender message that we were not out to destroy North Vietnam. We were supposed to say to them, "We just want to bloody your nose to get you to leave your neighbors alone."

We were supposed to say to the Thais, Koreans, Malaysians, and others that we would stand resolutely against the tide of aggressive communism. At the same time we were to say to the Indians and Japanese that our objectives were limited, our fear of broader war as great as theirs, our willingness to compromise greater than our adversary's.

I soon learned that my agency operated on the basis of more than a hundred "country plans"—a set of priorities, objectives, and programs designed for each country in which we operated. Each plan was based on what the ambassador, the U.S.I.A. chief, the intelligence experts, and the military analysts agreed was peculiar to and important about that country. It must be obvious to you that we lived with many conflicts of objectives from one country to another. We were required to carry propaganda water on both shoulders, and a little bit of it on the knees.

Yet, I took up with enthusiasm this challenge to communicate at large—to "tell America's story to the world." Imagine my great shock to learn that U.S.I.A. wasn't even communicating with the American people. I found that I had a well-staffed secretariat to handle the hundreds of letters that came to the director each day. Someone thought I was a bit nuts when I insisted on seeing regularly a sampling of this mail. When I looked at my first sample I understood why the secretariat might question my demand. Most of the public clearly was of the impression that the U.S. Information Agency was the place to which any citizen wrote who was having a problem finding something out.

A boy in Amory, Mississippi, wanted to know when the Beatles were coming to the United States again and where in Montgomery, Alabama, they were going to perform.

From Elizabethtown, Pennsylvania, a lad wrote: "I would like to find out some information about a girl. Her name is Nora Carroll. She lives in Lancaster, Pennsylvania. I would like to know how old she is now, how tall she is, the color of hair. What school she goes to, what grade she is in. I hope this won't be too much trouble to you. I guess that will be all."

And U.S.I.A. must be absolutely the favorite Washington agency of youngsters writing high school term papers. A student in Riviera Beach, Florida, wrote saying, "I have been assigned to do a report on the nationwide problem of prostitution. Any pamphlets, interviews, charts, accounts, book lists, articles, or statistics that you could send me would be greatly appreciated." And the wife of the mayor of a large California city wrote: "I would appreciate having any information you have available concerning testing to determine compatibility before marriage . . . I will be opening an introduction service and would like assistance in ways to match clients for marriage. I have enclosed $1.00 for samples of anything you may have that would be helpful."

I soon found out why U.S.I.A. was not communicating with the American people. It was the same reason for the lack of communications across international lines, and across ethnic boundaries in this country: fear, of one kind or another.

Congress had laid down certain prohibitions against U.S.I.A. communicating with Americans. There was one band of congressmen who did not want U.S.I.A. lobbying for public support for larger appropriations. It was one thing for a huge military-industrial complex to lobby to push the military budget over seventy billion dollars a year, but heaven forbid that anyone lobby in behalf of the dissemination of ideas and information.

But there was a larger fear that was basically political. There was the constant, and partly valid, fear that some party, or politician, would turn this huge propaganda apparatus to selfish political benefit. In my time, the great fear was that U.S.I.A. would make Lyndon Johnson look like a saint to the American voter. This fear constituted about as big a compliment as anyone could have paid to the prowess of U.S.I.A.'s propagandists!

Much that is wrong with the mass media today can be attributed to some kind of fear. Fear of controversy. Fear of advertisers. And most of all, fear of disapproval by the publisher's or editor's peer group—by the boys down at the club.

I also learned that many of our communications problems at U.S.I.A. flowed from the fact that millions of Americans do not appreciate the potency of words, the power of ideas. They cling to attitudes belonging to an era when we could say arrogantly, "To hell with the rest of the world and what it thinks about us. We can lick 'em all in the showdown."

This arrogance sometimes expresses itself in the notion that communications with the rest of the world consists basically of our telling other people what is good and right about us. We see little necessity to know what is good, different, and just about the acts and aspirations of other peoples. For example, we have spent hundreds of thousands of dollars telling the Nigerians what a great, generous, democratic people we Americans are. Yet, a bitter, murderous civil war has raged in Nigeria for a year, and I venture to say that most Americans can hardly give the name of the "country" that is fighting the Nigerian federal authorities.

Oh, our press carries reams of copy about the war in Vietnam. After all, *American* boys are involved in that struggle. But if as many people died today in the conflict between Nigeria and Biafra, so what? It is just so many more dead Africans.

I state it harshly, perhaps. But I do so deliberately. We have a terrible domestic crisis in this country because this provincial philosophy has governed the operations of so many newspapers. A journalism professor in Texas recently was telling me that he works summers on the copy desk of a newspaper in a good-sized Texas city. One night, he said, the editors were bemoaning the fact that there was just no news—foreign, national, or local. What could they use for a play story? Faces lit up when a telephone call told of a car crash nearby, in this newspaper's heavy circulation area, with six people killed.

When the first edition was brought up, the professor looked for the play story, expecting to read of the tragic accident. But some story of no import or interest carried the big headline. He scanned all the stories above the fold: no accident. Finally at the bottom of the page he found three paragraphs about the auto crash. He was incredulous. How could it be there when the editors were so happy earlier to have a story to put a bannerline on.

He understood when he got to the last sentence and read: "All the victims were Negroes."

It was this kind of indifference, of racially-colored judgment, that was responsible for the fact that the press ignored the race problem in America for decades.

I remember so well my first break as a journalist. When I was a young reporter, writing obituaries and the sort, an error in the work schedule left me with time to propose a return to my native South to write about what had changed in the lives of Negroes since World War II. What I wrote, in 1951, turned out to be a sensation—and largely because daily American newspapers had been too timid to deal with the subject. If you were a Negro, you almost had to rape or murder someone, generally white, to make the newspapers. And it wasn't just a question of the Negro trying to get in the newspaper. In this country the two best known Africans were Tarzan and Jane. As these articles appeared in the Minneapolis *Tribune,* the mail and the telephone calls poured in, many of them asking me to speak to this group or that.

As I journeyed to speaking platforms in rural Minnesota and the Dakotas, one thing got to be as regular as breathing: Someone would get up in the audience and say, "We don't have any race problem in our town; we don't have any Negroes."

Then I would try to explain that the problem doesn't exist in the presence or absence of Negroes, or any other "out" group; it exists in the heart and the mind. One only needs the presence of minority group members to make the problem manifestly obvious.

Today the press seems to sense a larger responsibility in these areas of social conflict and dislocation than was the case two decades ago. We have now a surfeit of newspaper copy and television treatment of the "race problem." There is, however, a rather vigorous debate as to whether this better serves the interest of justice and the nation than did the old policy of timid silence.

Whitney M. Young, Jr., director of the National Urban League, argues that Stokely Carmichael is primarily the product of a press that craves sensationalism and conflict. He says Carmichael's following consists only of a handful of Negroes and "about 500 white reporters." Allowing for an element of overstatement, I am afraid that Young spoke more truth than the press is willing to admit.

When Carmichael was virtually a nobody, some newspapermen noticed his facility for making inflammatory statements. And they made good copy. Very quickly, newspapermen and television interviewers everywhere were seeking out Carmichael to see who could relay to the public the most reckless utterances.

The press made Rap Brown a national figure in the same way.

The truth today is that someone who legitimately speaks for thousands of Negroes, who articulates their hopes and frustrations, can show up in most American cities and get no better than routine press coverage. But let a Negro show up who says: "If you don't do this or that we're going to burn down this damned town." I guarantee you he'll make front page headlines and all the TV shows.

Does this mean we need some kind of code to govern the coverage of riots and other racial disturbances? I say absolutely not. Who can develop what kind of code that tells a reporter or editor what he must do in a situation that carries all the variables of human behavior. What we need are reporters and editors with knowledge of what it is they are writing about; with some contact with the people about whom they write. No newspaper would think of having a labor reporter who did not have some intimate contacts and associations with the men of organized labor. An editor would scoff at the idea of carrying the reports of a police reporter who didn't hang around the police enough to know how they think, what their problems are, and figure out just whom to go to when he needed some reliable information. But you wouldn't believe the number of press people who write about racial problems in this country who don't know a thing about Negroes—or Puerto Ricans, or poor people.

The press is worrisomely representative of one broad characteristic of human society as a whole: We make scientific progress in the physical sciences, in the areas of technical knowledge, but very little progress in terms of our ability to control and turn to man's benefit this new technical knowledge, this scientific know-how.

Mindful of the geometric progression of new knowledge, many good newspapers today have science editors and reporters who are literally experts in the field—whose scientific knowledge is broader than that of many college professors. Editors assume, rightfully, that only a man who specializes, who reads constantly, who brings a depth of specific interest to the field, can really say to readers what they need to know and understand about man's efforts to conquer the elements around us and turn new light on the dark fastnesses of outer space.

But in the field of the social sciences—that area involving man's behavior that produces something close to anarchy on many campuses, an LSD fad at another college, a murderer in Memphis, explosive rioting in a Washington, D.C., or a Chicago—most editors assume that anybody strong enough to carry a pencil and bright enough to string one word after another is capable of going out to cover the civil rights story. I frequently put on the hat of a public speaker and have occasion to be interviewed by newspapermen in many an American city. I don't need tell you that the questions they are inclined to ask initially are all conditioned by my color—as if there is a basic assumption that race relations constitutes almost the sum total of a Negro's interest and knowledge.

And, oh how much is revealed by the questions some of these reporters ask! I see an appalling amount of ignorance, a remarkable array of prejudices revealed as some reporter says: "But you've got a better job than I have. Isn't that proof that Negroes are not discriminated against in this country?"

"But I understand more Negroes drop out of high school than whites do. Isn't this proof that Negroes prefer to live where they do with what they've got?"

When I think that these questions, and whatever part of the answers newspapers carry, constitute a basic source of social enlightenment of the citizens of scores of American communities, it is little wonder that the Kerner commission would conclude that the nation is in deep social trouble.

We need in this country something of the journalism of hope. It may seem a bit harder to make interesting than conflict, and it thus requires more skill, more work, and more money. But it is what we must produce if our dreams and ideals are not to be overrun by hopelessness and despair.

We can use today some of the philosophy expressed forty-six years ago by William Allen White. He wrote:

"Put fear out of your heart. This nation will survive, this state will prosper, the ordinary business of life will go forward if only men can speak in whatever way given them to utter what their hearts hold—by voice, by posted card, by letter, or by press. Reason never has failed men. Only force and oppression have made wrecks of the world."

Well, we live in a time when men are more inclined to rely on force and oppression than ever before. It is true in international affairs. It is true in our strife-torn cities.

If reason is not to fail men in our time, we of the press must give men the information, the knowledge, to sustain reason. We can do so by practicing the journalism of hope—and I do not mean a journalism that offers only the pre-sweetened pap of empty optimism. We can tell our readers the hard truths, the grim realities, and still have it add up to constructive journalism.

Consider that shocking report on malnutrition and hunger in the United States. A few church groups, foundations, and private citizens became concerned enough to assemble those grim facts about something that ought to shame us all. Now, where has the press been all this time? Why was it that some team of dedicated reporters did not put these facts before the people? Is it only that the work involved cost more than publishers were willing to pay? I doubt it. I rather suspect that it is easier to pretend that we are discharging our responsibility to orderly social change in this country when we quote both Whitney Young and Stokely Carmichael—thus, no need for the press to do any responsible crusading.

I see a new era, with some new worries, opening up for American journalism. We have seen a major effort by the Negro community to boycott the Memphis papers. This has serious economic implications for newspapers and their communities. It also raises the dangerous prospect of less information flowing into communities that desperately need more facts and fewer rumors. But this too is just part of the turbulence of change that we are charged with reporting and explaining.

Theodore F. Koop
Television: America's
Star Reporter

If anyone should consider it presumptuous for a broadcaster to take part in this centennial tribute to a great newspaper editor, I am not dismayed. For I am confident that William Allen White, with his probing curiosity and his zest for living each fresh day, would have been fascinated by the sweep and the potency of electronic journalism. In his autobiography he mentions the "miracle of radio." What would have been his reaction to the super-miracle of television? I can picture him appearing on the TV screen nightly as the "commentator's commentator," voicing his homely philosophy, putting difficult problems in perspective, and quietly waiting for the commercial to interrput his train of thought. What a Nielsen rating he would have enjoyed!

That is why I like the idea of Mr. White being in effect the sponsor—if I may use a hallowed word—of this seminar. It gives the media an opportunity to discuss both divergent and common problems. The techniques of newspapering and broadcasting differ greatly, but the aims are identical. Today I think all of us acknowledge that the print and electronic media, however competitive, complement each other. I would not want to live without newspapers, and I hope that editors feel the same way about news on the air. If it happens that the latest Roper survey shows that most Americans get most of their news from television, there are also figures that report unparalleled newspaper circulation.

But before I begin a treatise on the virtues—and perhaps a few shortcomings—of the modern, twentieth-century form of journalism, I should try to put into perspective the place of broadcasting as a whole in what we delight in calling our pluralistic society. We must start with one fact of life: broadcasting stations, unlike the press, are subject to government regulation—regulation that has its basis in the insufficient frequencies for all who might desire to enter the television and radio business. As you know, the Federal Communications Commission decides who is best qualified to receive a license and then, before granting renewal every three years, ascertains that the licensee has been serving the public interest. The Communications Act of 1934 forbids censorship of broadcast programs, but post-broadcast complaints find their way into a station's file at the FCC, to be reviewed when license renewal time comes around.

This review and the fact that the term "public interest" is general enough to be interpreted in many ways often lead broadcasters to refer to "regulation by raised eyebrow." For example, at the moment many broadcasting executives are disturbed by the action of two of the seven FCC commissioners in asking fifty-nine Oklahoma stations—their licenses are up for renewal—for detailed information about their news and public affairs programming. They especially inquired about the extent of programs dealing with racial problems. The two commissioners also invited the networks to report which of their recent news and public affairs programs were carried by Oklahoma affiliates. All these letters are unofficial in the sense that they were not approved by the full FCC, but what is a recipient to do—ignore the request or furnish the answers?

The FCC, incidentally, has put into effect a fairness doctrine that assuredly would raise the blood pressure of newspaper editors were it ever applied to them. It is designed to make certain that a station presents opposing viewpoints of controversial issues, gives a man opportunity to reply to a personal attack, and invites rebuttals to its editorials. What would an editor say if a government agency imposed these conditions upon his news and editorial columns? What would he say if he were ordered to give equal space to all candidates for a certain office? I can envision Norman Isaacs, for example, calling upon his freedom under the First Amendment and continuing to exercise his own best judgment in presenting a responsible, balanced publication. How broadcasters, equally fair-minded and responsible, envy his independence!

In talking about the role—or roles—of broadcasting in the United States today, I shall resist any temptation to analyze Professor McLuhan's thesis that the medium itself is the message. There is enough debate over television's social aspects without delving into McLuhan's mystique. Why should not television be accepted for what is is—a mass medium of communication?

That term has always been applied to newspapers, and rightly so. Because of its geography, the United States has no national newspapers such as blanket England. The three television networks, on the other hand, can simultaneously reach virtually all of the 94 per cent of American homes with TV sets. This nationwide focus of attention, be it for a pro football bowl game or the funeral of an assassinated President, is a catalyst that unquestionably is breaking down regional attitudes and attributes. Portland,

Maine, and Portland, Oregon, are becoming more and more alike. Their interests and reactions are all-American.

As FCC Commissioner Lee Loevinger has noted: "Television is an element of our culture because it shows things of common and universal interest. National culture is not found in museums or formed by graduate schools or universities. It is composed of common habits and patterns of living of people in daily activities, and of the common interest in entertainment, sports, news, and even advertising.

Television's massiveness—the size and spread of the audience— creates special problems for the broadcaster. He must reach persons of every level of education and of every social background. Most programs must interest the bulk of the potential audience, but programs also must be provided for smaller groups with diversified interests and needs. And it is heartening to note that these special programs—serious dramas, documentaries, even an occasional ballet—are finding receptivity by a continually increasing number of viewers.

To attract audiences to these outstanding events, it is first necessary to bring the more popular programs to them. I am reluctant to compare this situation with the farmer who frequently hit his mule with a two-by-four. It was necessary, he said, to engage the mule's attention. Roy Danish, director of the Television Information Office, expresses it in less colloquial terms:

"The one common denominator of our society's many interests is quite clearly entertainment, and given television's lineage and origins in the theatre, motion pictures, and radio, it is not surprising that both the most popular and most available elements in television are entertainment programs. It is the continued availability of entertainment that provides massive audience support. Just as broadcasters need this support to stay in business, so those who would use television to inform, to educate, to uplift, need a massive audience base to be heard at all. If a society's sights are to be raised through a mass medium, the society must first be brought to the medium."

Bemused broadcasters sometimes remark that "nobody loves us but the people." Criticism of television has become one of America's favorite sports—indoors or outdoors, depending on the weather. My distinguished colleague Eric Sevareid was recently moved to describe the highbrows who claim never to watch television but who are always most vocal in their objections to its programs. He said:

"There is, and always has been, a broad swatch of professional intellectuals who fear and detest anything new, particularly if it is adaptable to the pleasure of the great mass of ordinary people. This particular type of intellectual neither knows nor likes ordinary people. This is why they write about 'humanity' and not about persons. They are like the English Puritans who hated bearbaiting, not because it gave pain to the bears but because it gave pleasure to the spectators."

But the severest critics of television are the industry people themselves—the producers who seek greater imagination and creativity through the technological marvels of the art, the newsmen who covet an hour instead of fifteen or thirty minutes to report all the compelling events of the day, and the executives who must juggle income with the fantastic costs of program production. They are most conscious of their imperfections and their aims, and are a little awed by the fact that in twenty years they have reshaped the entire communications process.

Of all of television's manifold opportunities and responsibilities, my own view is that its most important single function is the dissemination of news and information. And I do not mean just daily showings of film clips of exciting events. Beyond the spot news of the day the broadcaster, like his brothers in the print media, has the duty of explaining events and putting them into perspective. Thus the documentary, a unique program form, is assuming increasing importance in network and station schedules.

Radio news achieved its stature with the advent of World War II, more than fifteen years after the commercial industry began; and it still performs a valuable service. Television news was nearly as slow in its development. At first many broadcasters considered it a novelty, just another form of entertainment. To present news programs they drafted announcers with honeyed voices and profiles that earlier might have graced Arrow collar ads. But professional newsmen, first recruited from newspapers, have gradually replaced these pretty-boys until today television is creating its own generation of trained reporters and editors.

In addition to journalistic competence, a TV newscaster must possess a nebulous quality that, for lack of a more precise word, might be called flair. He must have believability—the knack of putting the news across. I suppose the greatest compliment he can receive is the comment, "He sounds as if he knew what he's talking about." For he is not merely an impersonal by-line. Walter Cronkite and Huntley-Brinkley, for example, are the men who come to dinner in multitudes of homes; they are welcome friends of the family.

Television newsmen are the first to acknowledge that their programs, disciplined by the clock, cannot provide as thorough coverage of the day's news as a metropolitan paper. The number of words spoken in a half-hour newscast would fill only about three columns of type. Yet TV news has won tremendous popular acceptance. Not only does the Roper survey rank it as the prime news source for 64 per cent of adult Americans, but it also rates television first in believability. Although I unblushingly admit to prejudice, I think it is proper to give television the accolade of "star reporter."

Incidentally, in mentioning the Roper survey, I might digress from its news findings to report its result in other television matters. It found that an overwhelming majority—80 per cent—believe that "having commercials on television is a fair price to pay for being able to watch it." It listed three groups most critical of what they called "the bad effects of television on children," and I think you will consider them highly interesting: people who do not have a television set, people who have grade school education or less, and people who do not have children.

The impact of television news has never been more apparent than in the coverage of our immediate crises—the Vietnam war and the racial disturbances in American cities. It is not quite accurate to call the Vietnam conflict television's first war, for there was admirable film and voice reporting of the Korean fighting. But TV sets were fewer then, and this is the first war which the entire nation has been able to witness. Films taken only a few hours earlier bring home not only the horrors of battle but the searing effect on the civilian population of Vietnam.

This is not a pretty sight. Television has banished the glamor of war forever. People do not like what they see, and many want to stop seeing it. Letter after letter urges broadcasters not to show the blood of battle, because it is too awful—not to show Viet Cong villages being burned, because our troops would never do such a thing—not to report Allied failures and mistakes, because it is unpatriotic. Moreover, these complaints object to the lack of firsthand accounts of what goes on behind the enemy's lines—his campaign of terror and torture, his own mistakes and failures.

Unfortunately, American newsmen cannot take cameras and microphones into enemy territory, any more than they can erase the gore and the terror of the entire war and suddenly make the fighting antiseptic. They cannot turn it into a clean war. To be sure, they edit for taste. But they cannot black out the conflict and give their viewers the ostrich's confidence that it has gone away.

War coverage does avoid one great dilemma that presents itself in reporting an urban riot. The course of the Vietnam fighting is not changed by whatever is shown on TV screens in the United States. That may not be the case, however, with spot coverage of a racial disturbance. There is always the possibility that even the presence of television reporters and camera crews on the scene may generate further violence. Broadcasters in various cities have tried different methods of preventing such action. In some instances they have withheld all news of a disturbance for thirty minutes or so, until police can move in. Elsewhere, they have avoided live coverage and have shown film later. In many instances they have removed the camera crews if it appeared their presence was contributing to disorder.

None of these procedures, of course, is entirely satisfactory. In a forum before the American Society of Newspaper Editors, Richard Salant, president of CBS News, observed: "You can get a small, sporadic action and it can look like Armageddon, but it isn't. But if we don't give live coverage, we give rise to this question: If you're not covering this, what else are you not telling us?" Emmett Dedmon of the Chicago *Sun-Times* promptly noted that whereas Chicago television stations had delayed broadcasting inflammatory material, his city desk was deluged with telephone complaints that people had lost confidence in television because it was not carrying incidents which the callers themselves had witnessed.

The question also arises whether such extremists as Stokely Carmichael and Rap Brown should be allowed air time. As in the case of the Vietnam war, the activities of Carmichael and Brown would not cease just because they were not seen on television. But broadcasters appear to be generally agreed that during the tension of a civil disturbance, their air appearances should be minimal, if shown at all. The danger of further incitement is too great.

In these cases the broadcaster, like the newspaper editor, must make his own decisions, minute by minute, to fit immediate events. He cannot, like his critics, have the benefit of second-guessing. Television news is often live and thus does not even have the benefit of prior editing. The broadcaster stands on his best journalistic judgment, showing reportorial restraint but recognizing the necessity of giving his audience as much information as possible under the circumstances.

A sidelight on the problems of television riot coverage: In Washington, D.C., the district attorney has just subpoenaed, for grand jury study, all the broadcast scripts and all the film shot during the recent disturbances there. This has serious implications. If the D.A. can make his action stick, the Negro community might readily come to regard television as an adjunct of "the law," the medium would lose its credibility, and reporters and cameramen would have a difficult time covering Negro stories.

I should like to discuss one other phase of television journalism —the reporting of governmental affairs and the election process. What can be of higher purpose in a democracy where the people choose their officials and then monitor their performance to determine whether they merit re-election?

The television camera focuses on these representatives at work; it is the people's agent in the halls of government. Before it appear the President, the Cabinet, members of Congress, governors and mayors to account for their stewardship, often under incisive reportorial questioning. The camera still is not admitted to sessions of Congress or to meetings of committees of the House of Representatives, presumably the elective body closest to the people. It is generally permitted in Senate committee meetings, and thus poses a problem for broadcasters, as pointed up by the recent hearings on the Vietnam war before the Senate Foreign Relations Committee. Is it a greater public service to carry such a hearing live and in full during the day, before a comparatively small, largely feminine home audience? Or is it preferable to edit the hearing into an hour of highlights, to be broadcast during prime evening time? Each method has its journalistic and its public supporters. To those who object when a television network or station chooses to present an evening summary instead of the full hearings, I would suggest that very few newspapers carry the text of a thirty-minute speech, much less five or six hours of hearings. And if one television source carries the live committee sessions, competitors need not feel as strong an obligation to do so.

Both television and radio broadcasters recognize that their media have not been fulfilling their maximum capability of public service in an election campaign. This is because of the "equal time" provision in the Communications Act. News broadcasts and such regularly scheduled interview programs as "Face the Nation," "Meet the Press," and "Issues and Answers" are exempt. Where there are only two candidates for an office, there is little problem. But did you realize that there were a score of candidates for President in 1964? The prospect of providing, say, twenty half-hours of air time for as many candidates, whether serious or frivolous, is inhibiting to the broadcaster's desire to acquaint voters with the issues and personalities of the campaign.

Repealing this section of the law would make it possible for broadcasters to keep the campaign in perspective by concentrating on major candidates, just as newspapers do. Waiver of the law in 1960 made possible the Kennedy-Nixon debates, whose popularity was indicated by the fact that a total of about 115,000,000 people saw or heard at least part of at least one of the four meetings. The average television audience for all four debates was 71,000,000. By comparison, the peak audience of any political broadcast in 1964—the night before election —was only 16,000,000. Perhaps even more important than the large audience for the debates was the fact that partisans heard the other side, in contrast to their usual tendency of following only their favored candidates either at rallies or in broadcasts.

Broadcasters currently are urging Congress to waive that portion of the law again this year, so that major presidential and vice presidential candidates can appear both before and after the conventions, not only in debates but in special interviews or talks. The climate is not ready for complete repeal. (If I may interrupt myself for a brief commercial, I would urge all newspaper editors here to endorse this waiver concept. Many editorialized in favor of it in 1960, and I know that was an important factor in the congressional action.)

I cannot leave the subject of political broadcasting without touching briefly on two more aspects. The first is the networks' innovation on election night in making computerized forecasts of winners from the early returns in key precincts. Some politicians complain these announcements may affect the late voters in the West—whether to jump on the bandwagon or to favor the underdog, they do not seem to be sure. But all the responsible research has failed to show any correlation between these early predictions and the decisions of last minute voters. In any event, these complaints, meritorious or not, could be silenced by the establishment of a twenty-four hour voting holiday, with the polls opening and closing at the same instant from Maine to Hawaii.

The other aspect is editorializing for or against candidates. As with editorials in general, this is done by a comparatively small number of stations. But the practice is gradually growing, and many officeholders are unhappy about it, even though time is provided for rebuttals. Broadcasters cannot ignore the possibility that Congress sometime may try to ban such endorsements. Curiously enough, I think it would never occur to Congress to try to forbid similar newspaper editorials.

Radio and television are helping to provide a greater variety of community voices—both editorial and news—at a time when the number of newspaper voices is diminishing. To be sure, too many of the broadcast editorials still are on "safe" subjects, but here again it would appear that the older print medium has furnished the mold. Boldness hopefully will come with maturity.

The cost of television news programming cannot be overlooked —more than $1,000,000 to cover one space flight; $3,000,000 for last year's Middle East war, and well above $10,000,000 for the convention and campaign coverage of a Presidential election year. A station's news department is frequently not self-supporting; for the networks the news deficit runs into millions of dollars a year. Yet, despite the expense and the manifold technical problems, the great majority of broadcasters now accepts complete journalistic responsibility. The quality of the finished product is not uniform, but the resolve and the zeal are there.

What lies ahead for television and radio? They are at the very heart of the exciting communications revolution that is really just beginning. Talk to an electronics engineer, and he will tell you that within a few years your home will boast many or all of these elements: a large wall screen for television viewing, a videotape recorder and playback unit, radio wired into every room, cartridge music throughout the house, a facsimile machine to receive your daily newspaper, a picture telephone, and a teletype connection to a central computer library for a myriad of instant information. You may have your own portable TV camera to replace home movies. Satellites may bounce television programs directly onto your screen, bypassing local stations. Fantastic? Not at all. Much of this equipment could be operating today; the rest is around the corner.

What will you see on your ultramodern television screen? I venture to suggest you can still enjoy the *Red Skelton Show* and *Bonanza* and *Peyton Place*, or their successors, but I believe you will also find a marked increase in news and public affairs programs beyond the 20 to 25 per cent of current network scheduling. I believe you will be offered a greater diversity of program sources. Perhaps some will come from additional UHF networks, perhaps some from the proliferation of community antenna television systems. Educational stations, which have been largely shoestring operations to date, will be able to present more and better programs, thanks to congressional establishment of the Public Broadcasting Corporation. Above all, economics and governments permitting, you will be able to receive live programs from countries around the world.

This latter prospect is the most breathtaking, for it promises an international exchange of information and cultures with far-reaching potentialities. Developing countries can promote literacy by relaying educational programs to the most remote villages. Capitalism and communism can watch each other at work. Instead of the present teletype "hot line" between Washington and Moscow, satellite television can become an open world "hot line" for all peoples to see and hear and share—and hopefully understand.

I do not say that will come about tomorrow or next year or the year after. The technical problems of international television will be the easiest ones to solve. Conflicts of national interest, censorship threats, lack of financing—those among other things will slow the realization. But I believe with Wilson Dizard, of U.S.I.A., who wrote in his book *TV: A World View:* "Properly used, television can be the form of a new age of interdependence, the only mass medium fully capable of crossing geographical, cultural, and political barriers to link men and nations in an evolving world community."

Stan Freberg
The Freberg Part-time
Television Plan

I have been asked to bring what light I could to the under-developed area of television and the overdeveloped area of advertising. It is with the greatest of pleasure that I shall give vent on those subjects, although perhaps more violently than expected.

The title of my paper reads: "The Freberg Part-time Television Plan: A Startling, But Perfectly Reasonable Proposal for the De-escalation of Television in a Free Society, Mass Media-wise." Before explaining my thesis, however, it is necessary for us to re-examine the state of television. In doing so, the trick will be to keep from being biased, to keep from making snap judgments, and to keep from throwing up.

First, let us appraise the state of advertising in television, and secondly, the programming which interrupts it. Along Madison Avenue, the rumor persists that I am hostile toward advertising. Let me clear that up right now:

I am.

But then satirists are, by nature, hostile toward the things which infuriate them in society. In my case, this encompasses almost everything: From the trivial dumbness of pop-art collectors to the serious tragedy of the American political system. A random sampling of the things I find myself loathing with a fine passion over a twenty-four-hour period would include the A.T. & T., Governor Lester Maddox, doggie bags, black power, white power, Internal Revenue Service power, zip codes, laundry marks, women's heel-less shoes, plastic drinking cups, plastic squeeze-'em ketchup dispensers, champagne bottles with plastic corks, most modern architecture, most sports, all neon signs, all menus with photographic reproductions of your food (which it never looks like), Las Vegas, grand opera, Guy Lombardo, most underground movies, the way Bob Dylan sings, the way Lyndon Johnson talks, the way most people want to quit work at five o'clock, and Muzak. The only thing I detest more than Muzak is the apathy of the people who stand mute in elevators, including myself, and bear it instead of ripping it out of the ceiling with their bare hands. And the only thing I detest more than that is the role advertising plays in the mass media.

The Associated Press in a recent story referred to me as "Stan Freberg, satirist turned advertising man." They were wrong on two counts. One, satirists don't turn into something else. They're a special breed, trapped inside a special point of view forever. It would be as though you said, "Spot, Dalmatian turned German Shepherd." And two, I'm not an advertising man. If you don't believe me, ask any big agency on Madison Avenue. Still, I *appear* to be an advertising man because I write and produce commercials. One can understand the confusion of the Associated Press. But they're not as confused as I am. I have been known to kill an hour and forty minutes with a Diner's Club application, worrying over that little space that says "occupation."

What I am today is a humorist-satirist who keeps desperately trying to finish a book for Random House, complete a screenplay, record a new album for Capitol, and get an original Broadway musical based on American history into production, but can't because I keep working around the clock producing one advertising campaign after another. Why then do I stay in there, feeling the way I do? My critics, whom you can count on the fingers of the Mormon Tabernacle Choir, hasten to point out that the reason I stay in advertising is clearly stated in Latin on my letterhead. Under the Great Seal of Freberg, Ltd., is the inscription: *Ars Gratia Pecuniae*, or, "Art for Money's Sake." Well, I'll admit that's part of it, since I am in the business of selling bizarre ideas at (as my clients can tell you) a bizarre fee.

In talking to college students, I have asked them why they thought I went into the commercials business, and invariably *they* assume it was for the money. Or because "there's a lot of opportunities for advancement in that field," or, "advertising is glamorous and exciting!" True, I have experienced tremendous stimulation, creating some rather unorthodox advertising campaigns, which in most cases were successful in making the sales curve jump, to say nothing of the client. I have also managed to successfully unnerve several hundred account executives along the way. In my day I have made gray flannel turn white overnight. That in itself is an exciting sport. But the thought that I might have been motivated to go into this business not as an advertising man but as a totally outraged *consumer* rarely, if ever, occurs to them. Indeed, the main thing that has held me in advertising is the thing that got me into it in the first place. That is the challenge of proving daily that advertising does not necessarily have to be dull, insipid, nauseating, or irritating in order to communicate and thus sell the product.

Away back in 1956 I was a reasonably successful satirist making a decent living through television appearances, a CBS radio show, and periodic Capitol records which lampooned everything from *Dragnet* to Lawrence Welk and the late Senator Joseph McCarthy. As yet, I was untouched by the world of nervous marketing plans and more nervous account executives. My only connection with television advertising was the same as the average American's: I sat stunned and maddened at the ineptness of advertisers in their attempts to communicate with me. I wondered, "If we have to live with advertising, why doesn't someone try to make at least a portion of it bearable?" Advertising in that era was deadly serious stuff. There were no Volkswagen ads, no funny Alka Seltzer spots, no Sunsweet Prune lampoons.

As early as 1955, in Hollywood, I had proposed the Freberg approach to advertising, and my humorous scripts had been treated as though they had leprosy. Evidently, these vice-presidents had heard the expression, "Laughter is contagious," and misconstrued it. I, however, bravely continued to work among my contaminated scripts. It was thus in those days that I earned the title, "The Albert Schweitzer of Advertising."

Late in 1957 I brought in a pilot script at the request of CBS. It was fashioned after my CBS radio show of that year. During the course of the series I had managed to make the CBS building in New York tremble by doing skits on a fictitious Nevada city in which two hotels, the El Sodom and the Rancho Gomorrah, compete with each other. To the CBS executive's horror, I had the audacity to have written the commercials in the pilot show in a humorous manner. He said to me, "Satire is uncommercial enough in the programming end; God forbid we allow you to inject it into the commercials themselves. Furthermore," he continued, "your type of humor is really not very adaptable to the moving of consumer goods."

When I pointed out that I'd sold roughly five million satirical records to *somebody out there,* another vice-president said, "Well, those were record buyers, not consumers.

Transfixed by the clarity and power of that rationale, I walked out of CBS and climbed inside my 1957 Trojan Horse. Revenge was sweet when, nine years later, the CBS television network came to me to produce sixteen spots to promote their new 1966 fall schedule. They must have been temporarily mad. Confronted with a show like *Hogan's Heroes,* I gleefully announced to the country: "If you liked World War II you'll love *Hogan's Heroes!"*

But I digress. The point I had tried to prove to the long-since-gone programming man at CBS, and to advertising men—that the average viewer, treated as though he had some degree of intelligence, would, out of gratitude if nothing else, go out and buy the product—is, today, beyond reproach. The question I now raise, is: Have we reached the point of such commercial saturation, that *any* spot, funny or not, brilliant or bad, will soon fail to register anything?

Professor James Dykes, of the School of Journalism at the University of Kansas, quotes the great William Allen White, who said, some years back:

> Advertising is the genie which is transforming America into a place of comfort, luxury, and ease for millions. Advertising is the Archimedean lever that is moving the world. If things were done in another and elder age that advertising is doing now, a whole mythology would gather about it, and we should witness the birth of a young God—powerful, restless, indomitable and wise, dominating. He would flash in the sylvan glades of the want advertisements and disport himself in the sunny whiteness of a department stores' wide spaces. But what a god he would be! How beneficent, how omnipresent, how powerful!

Professor Dykes adds: "If Mr. White had lived to see this 'genie' grow into the giant that it has become today it would be interesting to speculate upon his evaluation of the role of present-day advertising."

You said it, brother! Mr. White had not yet seen the Ultra Brite toothpaste spots, the Head & Shoulders epics, or the knight in the suit of rented armor who recently rode through American living rooms hundreds of times a week. Omnipresent is right. When Mr. White died in 1944, he had probably never *seen* a television spot. The national advertising budget that year was something less than three billion dollars. Eleven years later, in 1956, when I entered the field, the national advertising budget was up to nine billion dollars. In 1968, it hit nineteen billion dollars, about nineteen times as much as is allocated for the poverty program. Proctor & Gamble alone spent $206 million for advertising in 1967. Of that, $196 million was its TV budget. (The word budget seems rather ludicrous in context with that mind-blowing allocation.)

This is no mere accident, and it didn't happen overnight. As the insatiable grasping of America's larger manufacturers swelled, not accordingly with the population, but out of all proportion, people were appropriately renamed (somewhere along the line) "consumers." In order to move this overwhelming stockpile of goods, the consumer had to be convinced that his mission in life was to *consume* and that he wanted and needed these things in abundance, whether in fact he did or not. To accomplish this, the volume of advertising obviously had to be increased, and the disciples of Hard Sell along Madison Avenue leaped to the challenge.

In their voracious zeal to sell, sell, sell, they began to irritate, irritate, irritate after the manner of their great leader, George Washington Hill, with his World War II slogan: L.S.M.F.T.! L.S.M.F.T.! This worked just fine until the novelty wore off and the listener suddenly saw the average radio commercial for what it was: Someone hollering at him. This resentment began building up. With the advent of television, it became possible to irritate, nauseate, and alienate the consumer visibily as well as audibly.

Lest we forget the kind of spot that started the great exodus from the American living room, let's refresh our memory with a splendidly revolting classic, the Carter's Little Liver Pills commercial.

It came up on a stern faced actor (Everyman's grandfather) in a white coat. The illusion was that he was at *least* a Nobel prize winning pharmacist. It was one of the few commercials I ever saw with a main title: "The Miracle of Your Liver Bile!" Then the man spoke: "Watch this laboratory demonstration! See? The fat globules in *this* flask are too big. They can't pass. *But* when liver bile is added . . . ." I shall spare you the globule by globule description of the action from that point. Its only gift to the American public was that it was shot in merciful black and white. In living color viewers would have tossed their TV dinners right there on the old Bigelow carpet.

I am reminded of the story of the man who took Carter's Little Liver Pills all of his life and lived to be 110. Three weeks after he was dead, they were still beating his liver to death with a stick.

That spot was one of many produced by the Ted Bates Company. The man responsible for the approach was probably their guiding chairman of the Board and misguiding light, Rosser Reeves. I once called Reeves "the dean of the gastrointestinal school of advertising."

Of course, in fairness, we mustn't judge all commercials by Mr. Reeves's ever-popular stomach acid and liver pill spots. We've come a long way since then. To illustrate how far we've come, there is a recent artistic triumph from Proctor & Gamble starring Ice Blue Secret Deodorant.

In scene one, the ever popular Katy Winters is seeing off on an ocean voyage perhaps the homeliest girl of the year. In her sensible tweed suit, horn-rimmed glasses, and frumpy hair-do, she confesses to Katy: "Frankly, I . . . . I worry about *perspiration!*" Out of Katy's purse comes a package of—how about that, folks!—Ice Blue Secret Deodorant. *Now* she ought to be able to meet some nice men, Katy tells her. In the next shot the girl is calling Katy ship-to-shore. Next to her stands the image of Ricardo Montalban, in Matson Line whites. But what's this? Miss Frump is in a strapless organdy, with her hair swept up by Mr. Kenneth, and no glasses. "Uh huh!" she giggles into the ship-to-shore phone, "every dance, Katy! Thanks to Ice Blue Secret!" Cut to the product (roll-on or spray).

Well, what are we to deduce from that enlightening commercial? It would certainly seem that that girl taking the ocean voyage had a lot more to worry about than perspiration, right? But wait! Ice Blue Secret Deodorant becomes a kind of "roll-on fairy godmother." If you are homely, Ice Blue Secret can make you appear beautiful! If you are shy and have no personality, it can get you handsome ship's officers. What's more, the girl in that commercial, after only a couple of nights with this deodorant, was able to go without her glasses! Marvelous! Let's take a look at one more "slice of life" from Proctor & Gamble, starring Head & Shoulders Shampoo.

A daughter is double checking last minute details for her wedding.

DAUGHTER: Let's see . . . bridesmaid gifts, invitations, and, Daddy, you've *got* to do something about that dandruff.

MOTHER: Poor Daddy. He's tried so *many* dandruff shampoos.

DAUGHTER: But he hasn't tried Head & Shoulders.

DADDY: *(Looking up from his paper)* Huh?

We cut to the shower with Daddy lathering up so as not to disgrace the bride. Suddenly we cut from the shower to the tail end of the wedding ceremony. Everyone is crying and milling about.

DAUGHTER: I'm so proud of my daddy.

DADDY: *(A quick glance at the shoulder of his tux)* You mean because of what Head & Shoulders did for my dandruff?

DAUGHTER: *Giggles and gives him a little squeeze. (Just where the hell her husband is is not explained. Obviously he has been shrewdly written out, thereby saving P. & G. a residual payment.)*

DADDY: I look at it this way. I haven't lost a daughter, I've gained a dandruff shampoo.

As they exchange stars in their eyes we cut to the product and fade out.

Isn't that beautiful? It is indeed a wonder we haven't developed a whole new kind of foot injury from people kicking in their picture tubes. Actually, there is little danger of this. Advertising has forced people to build themselves a special set of resistance reflexes, so that they can automatically block out insipid commercials mentally after the first viewing. In other words, the consumer has been beaten about the eyes and ears with the baseball bat of hard sell for so long now that he has developed what I call a cauliflower receptivity. No wonder it has become so hard to get the message through the scar tissue.

Of course, even if it did get through, it is doubtful if he would retain it longer than a split second, because it would be so insulting, or boring, or both.

There are several reasons why that Head & Shoulders spot is so uncommunicative. In the first place, it is about a distasteful subject—dandruff. If advertisers wish to be so unsubtle, let them use a medium like print, where people can be selective and flip right by it if it offends them. Viewers do not like being trapped in their living room. Even dandruff sufferers.

In the second place, it is embarrassing enough to watch grown people walking about discussing daddy's dandruff, without watching him suffer the indignity of having to bring it up again at his daughter's wedding.

In the third place, therefore, the whole thing is just so preposterous and unbelievable that people simply reject the whole premise.

In the fourth place, they must in the end be outraged that a great big grown company like P. & G. should spend millions of dollars beaming such trivia at them in all seriousness, expecting them to swallow it. It is an affrontery to their intelligence, and shows that the advertiser, in his greed to seize a corner on the market, has shown no regard for the dignity of man.

Now, I don't pretend that members of the viewing public sit there and psychologically break down their irritation, as I have just done. But their rejection is there just the same. Also, I don't mean to make such a federal case out of a dandruff commercial. It is the accumulative effect of such massive aggravation in the living room, however, that has built The Great Wall of Resistance to advertising.

Of course, you shouldn't just take MY word for it.

You should pick up a copy of the *Christian Science Monitor* dated August 18, 1967. One thousand readers responded to the *Monitor's* inquiry as to how people felt about commercials. The poll, entitled "TV Viewers Answer Back," revealed that 67 per cent wanted a broader range of selection in programming; 50 per cent did not favor the present system financed by advertising; 72 per cent found commercials annoying; 64 per cent found them not tasteful; 60 per cent considered commercials too frequent; 60 per cent did not find them entertaining; 49 per cent found them unacceptable; and finally, 46 per cent found them intolerable.

Of course, this is nothing new. Back in 1965, the North American Newspaper Alliance, one of our largest newspaper syndicates for more than forty years, conducted its own official large-scale sampling of the people's true feelings.

The poll revealed some interesting facts:

N.A.N.A. has conducted an enormous nationwide poll on television programming and commercials, and the most recent results from 5,200 ballots all over the country ought to open eyes along Madison Avenue, particularly among those agencies specializing in TV advertising. American television viewers' reaction to TV commercials is violent and certain, and no holds are barred in the N.A.N.A. balloting. Most viewers say they "simply can't stand any more commercials." Most unpopular ones appear to be the Ajax "White Knight," and "White Tornado," and the "Dash makes your washing machine clean like it's ten feet tall" messages. Crest Toothpaste is unpopular for the repetitious nature of its commercials.

The report goes on to name many other offenders.

"Well," one might ask, "if the people are as infuriated with these types of commercials as it appears, how do you explain the fact that a great many of these products have been successful at the sales level?"

According to "Freberg's Law," which I have been preaching for the last nine years now, the consumers have long since reached the point of commercial saturation. Thus, a major soap company, say, has to spend more and more to reach the poor consumer who is, in the interest of his sanity, slowly building an immunity to commercials, which forces the soap company to have to spend even more, and the consumer, accordingly, to build more immunity. Since advertising, then, like narcotics, must be taken in ever-increasing doses, it is easy to see why the annual costs keep soaring, until they have become what my friend Howard Gossage refers to as "a nineteen billion dollar sledge hammer to drive a 39-cent thumbtack."

Of course, Freberg, Gossage, and the readers of newspapers that take polls are all nuts. Right? Everyone in the ad "game" knows that. So that same year, 1965, the American Association of Advertising Agencies conducted its own study, later printed in *Sponsor* magazine. They really got to the bottom of it, all right. The facts uncovered in the Four A's study were hung with black crepe and discussed in the April 26, 1965, issue of *Sponsor*: "Agency management faces a 'tremendous problem, the monumental indifference of consumers toward most advertising,' William B. Lewis, Kenyon & Eckhardt board chairman, told last week's meeting of the Four A's. 'Any agency president or chairman, or any client president or chairman, who doesn't get goose pimples out of this evidence of advertising's minimal impact is kidding himself,' Lewis said."

In the same issue, Paul C. Harper, Jr., president of Needham, Harper & Steers, points out that the Four A study revealed, "The public is able to categorize, either favorably or unfavorably, only about 16 per cent of all the ads it is conscious of being exposed to. That means that 84 per cent of the ads noted did not evoke enough response from the average consumer to let him categorize them in one way or the other. What a way to die!"

Mr. Lewis and Mr. Harper act as though they are just discovering this fact of life. I have been hollering about advertising's "minimal impact" for years, but in many quarters I was written off as a loony. I could have saved the Four A's an awful lot of trouble and expense if they had just *come* to me and asked me.

On the bright side, of course, one doesn't really have to "die" with your ads, as Mr. Harper puts it. One needs only to know how to speak to another human being, in terms that will interest him, and you *will* communicate—not the eight hundredth time around, but the very first time he hears your message, and each time thereafter. I know it is possible, because I do it every day. On the other hand, some companies, in lieu of being able to bring off this elementary trick (companies like Proctor & Gamble, Bristol-Myers, and General Foods), have a counter-device for reaching the people. It is called *money*. Hurling it about, as though it were going out of style, they use what I call the "Invasion of Normandy" technique, with wave after wave of commercials striking at the viewer's head each evening of his life. He tried hard not to listen, but the dead commercials keep piling up on the front of his forehead until the tanks finally push in right over the tops of them and establish a beachhead in his brain.

This, obviously, accounts for the fact that even though these products infuriate people with their advertising messages, they can eventually enjoy success at the sales level. It's the Pavlovian dog experiment all over agin, but played with people instead of beagles. It isn't really advertising; it's brainwashing.

It would indeed be interesting to make someone like Bristol-Myers or Proctor & Gamble try to pull it off with only a couple of million dollars, as the Sunsweet Prune Company or Jeno's Pizza did, instead of the aforementioned two hundred million. It would mean, necessarily, a crash course in communications.

Advertising's primary function is to communicate. And yet, it would be hard to find an American industry that, for the most part, understands less about the art of communications than the advertising industry (with the possible exception of the CIA). If you think I'm exaggerating, I invite you to flip through any issue of the *Saturday Evening Post* or *Life,* or simply spend an evening glued to American television and watch, *really* watch and listen to an evening's worth of advertising. Fortunately for the consumers, they don't listen. Most of the time they simply walk out of the room. A testy Chicago account executive once told me that this was simply not true. "People *love* commercials," he insisted. I wonder if he has ever heard of the troubles heaped upon the city of Toledo a few years back. The town was alarmed to discover that the city water level dropped alarmingly at periodic intervals on a weekday evening. Especially on Tuesday, between 8 and 8:30. A further check revealed that the dropping of the water level coincided precisely with the network break of *I Love Lucy,* which everyone was watching at once. The beloved commercials hit and the people fled to the bathroom as one man.

Nevertheless, advertisers across America continue to delude themselves into thinking that a viewer will sit enthralled for the full amount of the client's allotted commercial time, out of respect for the excruciating amount of money paid for this air time. The sponsor who enjoys this type of Proctor & Gambolian thinking is obviously smoking opium. But, unfortunately, most of the time his agency does very little to help him kick the habit.

And so we have the answer as to why most television commercials are so dreadful and uncommunicative. Reduced to its simplest terms, the problem is compounded thusly: The average client, at a loss as to how to communicate his product to people, hires an advertising agency to show him, but still clings to hard sell as a child to a security blanket. His agency, if it *does* know how to communicate, rarely deems to fight for anything fresh, wild, inventive, or artful for fear of rocking the boat and/or their 15 per cent.

From where I stand, it seems terribly obvious that if an advertiser wishes to break through the mediocrity barrier, he dare not be anything *but* artful. By the "mediocrity barrier" I refer, of course, to that enormous bulk of audio-visual rubbish which comes spewing forth from the mass media, to the tune of billions of dollars a year, somehow passing for creative advertising. Perhaps, in all fairness, rubbish is not the proper word. Perhaps *garbage* is the proper word.

One way to get through to people is by satire.

I have been asked why, in many of my commercials, do I seem to kid advertising so much? It is because I find it stimulating to satirize Madison Avenue right there in the old lion's den. That is, to use advertising itself as an arena in which to kid advertising. As I said in a recent article in the *Variety Annual;* "It is as though one would use Dodger Stadium for a rally in which to protest baseball, while making Walter O'Malley pay you for doing it. The ace up my sleeve, of course, is that if there is anyone more outraged than Freberg at the insipid level of most commercials, it is the general public."

When a company like Jeno's Pizza comes along and uses its minute of time to parody the bad breath and deodorant commercials, the home audience is at first incredulous, then delighted to discover that someone in advertising obviously hates the same kind of ads *they* do.

So the commercial is functioning on three levels: (1) It succeeds as an entertaining commercial unto itself; (2) it manages to harpoon the very kind of commercials people most detest and therefore helps blow away that approach on a gust of ridicule; and (3) it creates such good will for the pizza company that it cannot help but benefit at the point of purchase, a condition which currently prevails all over America.

A commercial I wrote for Cheerios is another example of using advertising to lampoon advertising. The Cheerios division of General Mills was having difficulty reaching adults and retained me to suggest a more adult approach. When the first Excedrin commercials interviewing "real life" people assaulted us, I leaped to the typewriter and came up with this little slice of life. It employs the same brilliant actress, Naomi Lewis, but was produced five years earlier than the pizza spot.

Writers who have attempted to chronicle and analyze my work have pointed out that from the beginning in 1956 one element is usually present—honesty. Of course. That is my secret weapon. If you examine the advertising of the 1940's and early 1950's, you will soon discover that honesty was something not overly used by Madison Avenue. It was as though they had spent thirty years setting me up for the payoff. I'd like to mention two radio spots (one for Chun King Chow Mein and one for an airline) and a television spot for a prune company which dish out honesty in almost frightening amounts. At least they sure scared the clients pretty good.

Looking for a real moment of truth in advertising, I have said, is about like looking for Howard Hughes. You know he's around somewhere, but when is the last time you saw him with your own eyes in living color? In case you didn't know, the Chun King Company's sales went up 40 per cent from that campaign and its owner sold it last year to Reynolds Tobacco for sixty-four million dollars. Pacific Airlines went, overnight, from the world's most invisible airline, to international acclaim. They made *Time, Newsweek,* AP, UPI, the *National Observer,* and dozens of other papers and magazines from Germany to Australia. Huntley and Brinkley were so moved by the campaign's honesty that on their NBC news show they held up a New York *Times* ad I had written to go with the radio spot. If the airline hadn't merged with a more conservative and less courageous airline, which stupidly suspended all advertising during the merger, there's no telling what it could have accomplished. We'll never know. One thing we *do* know, however, is what plain honesty of approach did for the Sunsweet prune people after years of being wrinkled and unloved. They will show you their sales curve upon request.

I mention three final examples of spots which spoof various kinds of advertising. The first is a radio spot for Chun King, which sells it as though it were a Detroit automobile, utilizing that familiar and thinly veiled attempt to appeal to a man's masculinity. The second spot is a television satire on movie trailers, made for Banquet Frozen Foods (there's something very fitting about using Hollywood movie techniques to sell turkey). And finally, my latest TV commercial for Jeno's Pizza Rolls. Almost everyone has seen the Lark commercial it parodies, but not everyone was as outraged as I that the Lark Company lifted the music from both Rossini and *The Lone Ranger.*

I sometimes get to feeling like the Sorcerer's Apprentice, who could never finish tidying up. If a few of us manage to make some small corner of advertising bearable, with a dozen entertaining commercials for, say, Jeno's Pizza, Volkswagen, Alka Seltzer, American Airlines, and Sunsweet Prunes, the Ad Establishment, in their infinite ineptness, will have produced a hundred lousy ones before we can get ours out of the lab. And if I were somehow able to negotiate with a group of elves, who would work through the night and help me create *five hundred* commercials that were a joy to behold, I know that as surely as the sun came up Madison Avenue would have somehow unleashed upon us *five thousand* horrendous spots in which an army of white knights, perspiring actors, and leering toothpaste models would come riding and brushing and foaming and deodorizing their way into our living rooms, until not even Head & Shoulders Shampoo could wash away the memory of the assault upon our sensibilities.

What then, can be done? Anything?

I intend to try. It takes a Trojan Horse to teach a Trojan Horse, and that's what I hope to do in conducting classes at, appropriately, the University of Southern California.

The kind of soft-sell advertising I advocate can, in the end, become the hardest sell of all, by merely meeting the American public half-way and for a fraction of the cost. If I can teach that to some brilliant boy who may manage to infiltrate the ranks of Proctor & Gamble and end up fifteen years from now as the advertising manager, we may yet see some *real* relief in the living room.

But, who can wait that long? Saul Steinberg, the great satiric artist, cannot. Recently, while looking at *The Dating Game* or something equally deep, he picked up a container of black paint, and swiftly painted out his picture tube. Since the audio portion continued to assault him from behind the blackened window, he pulled the plug from the socket and nailed it to the wall. Not all of us are emotionally equipped to deal with television in this courageous and straightforward manner. As something in between Mr. Steinberg's *coup de grace* and the alternative of enduring television as it now exists, I offer a possible way out for the industry, and the audience: The Freberg Part-time Television Plan: A Startling, But Perfectly Reasonable Proposal for the De-escalation of Television in a Free Society, Mass Media-wise.

There's a lot more wrong with the old tube than just being assaulted by commercials. Right? The general level of programming offered us by the three major networks and the independents doesn't seem to be any better than it was five years ago. Maybe it's getting worse. In all fairness, though, how can we expect every program to be as profound as *The Flying Nun?* As uplifting as

Joe Pyne, as witty and hilarious as *I Dream Of Jeannie,* or *Good Morning World?*

Even if you could bring back such evergreens as *My Mother the Car,* or *It's About Time,* could you fill all the hours with such really good shows? It's doubtful. There just isn't enough top-level talent around.

The networks are forever wailing about the lack of real play-wrights. "Not enough Paddy Chayefskys, not enough Rod Ser-lings," they cry. And what if there were? Could you expect enough real actresses like Lee Radziwell to be available to fill the roles?

You can see the problem. So tell me this: Where is it written in blood that all waking hours of every single day must be filled up to the orthicon with television programming? Where is it engraved in stone that just because the hours are *there,* they must be sold? (Especially those evening hours chopped up like so many pieces of beef, by the networks, and named, appropriately, "prime" time.) If television is spreading its programming too thin, and its commercials too thick, while our minds slowly turn into rutabagas from trying to find some meaning in it all, let us reason together. The Freberg Plan would call for an immediate de-escalation of programming and commercials. Henceforth, America could watch television only three nights a week. That way the networks could weed out the deadwood and consolidate just the cream of their programs into Monday, Wednesday, and Friday. (It is just possible, of course, that when they finished weeding out the deadwood, they would end up staring at a test pattern. But I'll let that pass for the moment.)

Here we go:

MONDAY: Television as usual.

TUESDAY: The set goes black, but one word shines in the center of the screen: *Read!*

WEDNESDAY: Television as usual.

THURSDAY: The set goes black again, but this time we see the word: *Talk!*

FRIDAY: Television as usual.

SATURDAY: The words: *Unsupervised Activity!* appear on the tube.

What happens Sunday? You may well ask. We have to have somewhere to lump all those leftover commercials, don't we?

Think of it! Twenty-four glorious, uninterrupted hours of advertising! A veritable cavalcade of all they hold dear at the Harvard Business School! A salute to the mouthwashes, dog foods, aspirins, and deodorants that have helped to give us "the good life"!

If the prospect of such a Sunday does not appeal to you, you could always break it up with some extracurricular activity, like going to church. You remember church—that funny looking building with the pointy roof? No doubt people will have to be re-introduced to this ancient custom. The same way they will have to be re-introduced to their family when the lights come up in the living room on Tuesday, Thursday, and Saturday. We shall all have to help each other through the difficult withdrawal period. *Read* and *Talk* will pose no problem after a few days. It will all come back to us, like riding a bicycle.

But *Unsupervised Activity* could be sticky. What will Rap Brown take that to mean? Having read it, could he control himself? Maybe it should just say *Love,* on that day. But then, could Helen Gurley Brown control herself? There are many problems attendant to my proposition: What would *TV Guide* print on the blank pages every other day? Would they hang in there with me and also print *Talk* and *Read?* Or would they chicken out and sell the pages to some pitted prune company? It has been suggested that in order to facilitate my de-escalation plan, I be drafted into some position of electronic authority. I say to you that I do not seek, nor will I accept, the presidency of the CBS Television Network.

Bosley Crowther
Magic, Myth, and Monotony:
A Measure of the Role of Movies
in a Free Society

Make no mistake about the movies. In pursuing an examination of the functioning and effects of mass media in a free society, we must commence with a clear understanding that the movie medium is essentially engineered to provide the people with entertainment, indulgence, and escape.

This may seem a dogmatic statement—and perhaps a platitude —to ask you to accept at the outset of this discussion, especially since we are hearing so much nowadays about greater expansion and maturing in certain areas of film. But I have found it unwise and deluding to tackle movies with the idealistic thought that we can find in their commercial organization and production some ardent impulse to make them flow into forms that will have social purposes and values of an educational and soundly humanizing sort.

The prime aim of movie-makers is to catch the customers, to provide them with distraction and enjoyment by means of representations that conform to the customers' calculated prejudices and interests or their tolerance for surprise, and thus send them forth contented that their tastes and intelligences have been satisfied. The prime aim of movie-makers is to give you what they think you want—you being a thousand million people in this country and all over the world.

I am not being critical, at this point. I am not trying to denigrate and taunt a great device of communication that serves a recognized purpose in a difficult world. Keeping the natives contented in their established environments has always been a function of merchants, as well as governments. And surely exercise of the privilege of seducing one's fellow man—or woman—with distracting enticements is respected in a free society.

But we are not here to justify movies as ingenious commercial enterprise. We are here to assay the marginal service they are doing and have done over the years in bringing more than entertainment to people—in bringing enlightenment and enrichment to lives that are presumably needful of these felicities in a crass society. And we are here to explore the possibilities and likelihood of this medium doing more to expand the awareness of people and help them live more fully and productively in the years ahead.

Now I must note that by this presumption of a function for movies above and beyond the simple one of giving entertainment,

we are putting ourselves in the way of having to make and support value judgments that may tax our logic a great deal more
than we suspect. For I have to remind you that we are not coming
to this question of the role of movies in a free society as though
this were the first time the question had ever been asked. Since
the very beginning of movies, earnest people have solemnly inquired what are the effects of this medium and what are its social
responsibilities.

Preachers and educators, social scientists and critics, have asked
what are the movies doing to the people—or *for* the people. Are
they helping to uplift and educate? Are they providing something
more than entertainment? Are they providing *wholesome* entertainment? That is the word!

I bring up this point very early because I want to establish the
fact that the movies are probably the most closely examined and
frequently challenged medium we have. Although they are under
no obligation by their cultural nature to communicate fact or
truth, as presumably is the press, and they are certainly under no
compulsion to perform the responsibilities of preachers and teach-
ers in leading people in the paths of righteousness, they have been
constantly called upon to perform these functions and assume
these responsibilities. The movies have been candidly expected to
be everything from a truant officer to an art.

Therefore, I put it to you that we must proceed with caution
and care in defining our expectations of this medium, if we mean
to be reasonable and fair. And we must also be sharply realistic
in recognizing what movies actually are.

At the risk of being somewhat preceptorial, I would like to
make a hasty review of the history and expansion of this medium,
most of which has occurred in the lifetime of many of us here.

When movies were first exhibited to the public, they were
magic, sheer magic—only that. They were an experience so novel
and amazing that the thrill of looking at them—of seeing pictures
actually moving before one's eyes, out of context from all experience of nature—was all anybody wished. Those were indeed the
days when the medium—just the medium—was the message. That
was enough. Thousands—even millions—of people were fascinated by the magic of random images moving on a screen.

But the novelty of mere movement didn't last long. Repetitions
of railroad trains rushing at you or school girls skipping rope or

factory workers coming out of factories soon became quite monotonous. Thus occurred the first indication of a phenomenon that has been persistent in the commerce of the screen: the pertinent peril of transition from magic to monotony.

How to use the magic medium to provide the public with something that would entice and maintain its interest was the problem of the inexperienced men who operated the funny little cameras. And, of course, they soon came up—quite by chance—with the telling of little stories that were essentially myths.

Folk stories they were—simple fictions right out of the cheap literature that was familiar, understood, and indeed demanded by the great majority of Americans. The magic movies became a mechanism for manufacturing and communicating myths—the myths of their fictitious contents and the myths of the heroes and heroines they evolved.

I think it safe to guess that 99.44 per cent of the movies made in the United States—and in the rest of the world, for that matter—since *The Great Train Robbery* have communicated myths of one sort or another. They may have been gross myths, or they may have been myths that came so close to the romantic ideals, heroic concepts, and wishful thinking of the great middle-class that most of us were delighted and moved by them and regarded them as revelations of truth. Or they may have been myths of such conspicuous and charming fantasy, such as the films of Charlie Chaplin or Walt Disney, that we found joy and reassurance in them.

There is no need to run a lengthy recount of the formulae of these myths—the convention that the good guys beat the bad guys in every crucial showdown of strength; that the good girl gets the good guy away from the bad girl, in the end; that every American soldier is basically a hero; that our country always wins its righteous wars. I challenge you to analyze any movie—any fictional movie, that is—with rare exceptions, and not find it a compound of a convenient and comforting middle-class myth.

Even those films which we have called documentaries, because they have appeared to organize and show us facts, and those obsolete items known as newsreels have been generally tinctured with myths because they have propagandized along lines of wishful thinking or they have mainly catalogued the happier aspects of our lives, such as beauty contests and horse races.

The screen has rarely been a conveyor of trenchant truth—of the real natures contained in men and the frequent injustices and ironies of society as they exist.

And even if there did come a film maker who wanted to manifest such things—who wanted to shock and disturb the preconceptions and the illusions of the middle class—we have had laws and regulations to restrict and control exposés. The mechanisms of statutory censorship by which the movies (and *only* the movies) were rigidly bound in this country after 1915—right down to within the past few years—kept the film makers from putting forth concepts that were really anything more than myths.

Indeed, I have often wondered, if we had had no statutory censorship—if anybody had been free to manufacture or merchandise any sort of film he wished—I have wondered if we would not still have had pretty much the same sorts of films—the same purveyance to a middle-class market, with its prejudices and tastes— as we did. For the Screen Production Code, which was adopted to regulate the output of Hollywood—to force it to accept moral strictures—was the consequence of reaction to the pressures and demands of citizen organizations that insisted upon their middle-class myths.

The defense of the code during its dominance was that it enforced some social values on films. But it did not do that. It simply forced a nervous adherence to the parochial canons of its administrators' tastes. For instance, they thought divorce, abortion, or miscegenation were not respectable. Therefore these things could not be shown as advantageous in a movie, and they could only be suggested in the most carefully guarded terms. There were dozens of other obfuscations of reality supported by the code.

I am not saying that there weren't some good movies—some very good, entertaining ones—made under these restraints of middle-class taste and regulations. But for all their glints of realities—as in *The Grapes of Wrath,* for instance, or in the ironies of a *Citizen Kane*—they were pragmatically designed to arrive at resolutions that perpetuated sentiments and myths.

So the first burst of sheer movie magic was followed by a long period of profitably merchandised myth, which only showed its mechanical obsolescence and its aesthetic monotony when radio came along. The magic and myths of silent movies were sufficient all through the First World War and into the 1920's. Then the sounds and voices that came out of that little radio provided the public with a new kind of magic, and the monotony of movies without voices crept in.

I don't suppose many of you know this, but the movies were in a calamitous state—virtually dying for lack of attendance—when they were miraculously saved by the magic of sound. The fortuitous injection of talking movies brought a new aesthetic dimension and excitement to the screen. Attendance boomed, even though the Great Depression soon followed. The rotation from magic to myth occurred again. For even though many new subjects and devices of story-telling were allowed by dialogue and sound in movies, the contents continued to be myth. Poor Clark Gable married rich Claudette Colbert in *It Happened One Night.* Scarlett O'Hara regained Tara in *Gone With the Wind.*

I have dwelled on this historical rotation of magic, myth, and monotony because it does represent the basic pattern of the cultural and commercial progress of films. And its cyclical swing has been commanding right down to the present day.

What happened when a totally new magic called television came after the Second World War? It completely pre-empted the public's time, and quickly exposed the monotony of the conventional, repetitious theatrical films.

Most people assumed television was a new medium. It wasn't at all. It was and is motion picture projected in the home instead of in a theatre. True, the material projected by this means and the commercialized programming of it is somewhat different from the material and techniques of movies projected in theatres, and it is given the distinguishing name of Video Broadcasting. But it is movies, all the same, and its fascination lay at first in its magic —in the marvel of being able to sit at home drinking beer, eating pretzels, and watching movies for free.

As Alfred Hitchcock once said: "The invention of television was like the invention of inside plumbing. It did not essentially change the impulses of the individual. It simply made the accomplishment of the impulse more convenient and comfortable."

I assure you, good taste and critical judgment of the mass audience had nothing whatsoever to do with the encouragement given television. If good taste and critical judgment had ruled, the device would have died aborning. It was simply the magic of the thing.

But again the theatrical movie lost its audience to an alarming degree, and again it was saved from disaster only by the chance uncovering of another magic of its own. That was the fascination of the giant, pseudo-three-dimensional screen, which allowed for the projection of images of a massive and thrilling size. This device quickly captured public enthusiasm, and its felicities were spread through several large-screen techniques of a nature that induced the making of mammoth spectacle films.

So again through mechanical magic the theatrical screen was miraculously saved from what was, by turn, becoming the monotony of TV. But it was notable that only an occasional movie—maybe one out of five—aroused public interest and enthusiasm to the point where it became a hit.

This new aspect in the rotation, this discovery that the incidence of theatrical hits—money-makers—was reduced by the contention of the also myth-projecting TV, caused dismay in the ranks of movie-makers and movie merchants, and they diligently sought to change or spice up the content of movies so as to pull the customers out of their homes.

One such attempt was the costly production of bigger and grander spectacle films—which, of course, were but further penetrations and projections of the platitudes of myth. Another was the exhibition of carefully picked, foreign films which had bold and uncommon dramatic content and were usually laced with surprising discoveries of sex. These brought on stern action by the censors, and this led film importers to bring court actions against statutory restraints. They were successful, and the barriers of censorship were progressively broken down.

In turn, American film makers injected their films with more elements of sex and compelled what we called a liberalization and now virtually an abandonment of their production code. Customers were attracted. A new series of myths about sex was launched. And the redundance of entertainments of this nature was headed toward another rotation of monotony.

As I say, I have dwelled upon this pattern—this cyclical flow of films—because I know this is a fact of movie commerce that no immediately foreseeable changes are likely to break. Right now we are seeing television competing with theatrical films by presenting home viewers with movies of comparatively recent vintage and quality. This is indeed an amazing and amusing irony: the Box making capital of the relics of its older and more eminent peer.

The already evident rejoinder of theatrical film makers is to come out with even bigger, more elaborate, more myth-pushing spectacle films, as, for instance, an extraordinary line-up of big musicals. Also evident is a move by producers to bring a new magic to the theatrical screen by adapting some of the multi-image techniques that were so sensational in film exhibits at Expo 67.

While in Hollywood recently I was given glimpses of two almost finished films that use uncommon and pictorially dazzling compositions and sequences of many images piled together at the same time within the panel of the large screen. The purpose is to compress information in these quick composites and multiply the intellectual and emotional effects. Other films using these techniques are being started. So perhaps here we go again.

What I wish to make clear by this insistence on the cyclical pattern in the history of films is the significant fact that mechanical innovation more than any essential improvement in dramatic content and social philosophy has accounted for the continuation and apparent progress of the commercial movie in our free society.

Caught between the fundamental cultural pressure of the mass audience for entertainment that is fashioned on myth and the constant demands of a galaxy of theatres for more and more product that they can merchandise, the never too intensely philosophical film makers have been prevented from exercising their skills on precisely true or bravely penetrating dramas. They have been pushed too often in the direction of mediocrity and thus eventual monotony.

This is the case with the great bulk of our movies—and it is this great bulk, of course, which has spread its coating of myth and deception over our willing society. The great majority of our American movies and many of those we have imported from abroad have done nothing more than assist our self-indulgence and support our eternal optimism and complacency.

If any one charge of malfeasance and culturally criminal negligence can be brought against the movies, it is that they have failed to present us and pervade us with realization of our true selves and of the world in which we live.

How much have movies really shown us and told us of the complex nature of the mind and the impulses of man? How much have they informed and enlightened us about the horror and futility of war? How fairly and comprehendingly have they hinted at—much less dramatized—the existence and the monstrous inequities of the race conflict in the United States?

As for the complex nature of the mind and the impulses of man, I would say and repeat that what the movies have given us has been largely a reflection of our comfortable middle-class myths. Man is often cruel and villainous, full of selfishness and greed. But that sort of man invariably gets his comeuppance. The good man—the man for all seasons, or maybe just for the football season—prevails.

Even Citizen Kane, who is probably the most complex and challenging character ever contemplated in an American film, was shaped for us as an arch and ambiguous monster for whom understanding and sympathy were developed only through the middle-class fixations that he was industrially ambitious and he was in love with a sled when he was a little boy.

Our few and tentative explorations into the dark, subconscious chambers of the mind—which is an area, of course, that is known by scientists to be most productive of the vital impulses of man—have been mainly in the nature of melodramas, science-fiction, almost, the best of which would probably be Hitchcock's *Notorious* and *Psycho,* and the worst of which, some of those mad-doctor things with Vincent Price.

And to show just how antipathetic our mass audience would likely be to any American film that honestly invaded the most noxious and noisome chambers of a troubled mind, I cite you the general indifference and even hostility in this country to the series of brilliant Swedish films made by Ingmar Bergman, in which he explored several aspects of psychopathy.

Particularly, I ask you to consider the disgust that was indicated by many people who did give brief support to Bergman's recent *Persona* and his earlier *Through a Glass Darkly*. These were films in which he probed sexual and psychotic aberrations—incestuous and lesbian impulses. Revolting, too many people said.

This reminds me of a story of my old friend, that titan of

American film production, Louis B. Mayer. Someone spoke of lesbians to him one time, and he demanded to know what was a lesbian. The person, a bit astonished at this naïveté, tried delicately to explain. Mayer demanded a clearer explanation. When the friend told him explicitly what lesbians are and what they do, Mayer snorted in absolute indignation. "I don't believe it!" he said. "Nobody would do *that!*"

Well, I must say, I don't suppose there are many people in Hollywood now who don't know what a lesbian is. And from some of the movies we've been seeing lately, I'd guess they even know what lesbians do. But I can assure you that the pathetic perversion which is covered by the term will not be dissected in an American movie as sensitively as it is in Mr. Bergman's pictures. And even if it were, the film wouldn't have much chance with the American audiences, outside of the metropolitan and university areas.

We are interested in sex—oh, yes—in movies, but it has to be what Mr. Mayer again called "nice, clean, *wholesome* sex," like Bonnie giving her pure, white body to a temporarily impotent Clyde, then feeling romantically frustrated and having to content herself with Clyde's left-behind pistol—a smack of Freudian symbolism that not too many wholesome people got.

I have often criticized too much sex in movies, when it was dragged in for mere sensation's sake. I have never criticized it when I felt the purpose and the achievement was to use it to comprehend and reveal the genuine appetites or hang-ups of characters, as was done in such films as the Swedish *Dear John* and the Anglo-Irish *Ulysses.*

As to the impact of showing sex in movies, or playing around with sex themes, I feel it is better when these things are treated frankly than when they are treated with sly suggestiveness and peek-in-the-bedroom leers. I think the way the affair of the young man and the older woman in *The Graduate* is handled is one of the more honest, mature, and moral details I've ever seen in an American film. Here we jolly well know what is happening, we are made to sense the physical sloppiness of it, and we are led to realize the boredom of the woman and the significant disgust of the young man. I have been greatly heartened by the way a myth is put forth and exposed in *The Graduate.*

My concern about too much sex in movies—too much phony,

clumsy, leering sex, that is—is that it is simply artless and tasteless and as gauche as someone using dirty words. It's like kids ogling nudie postcards, a juvenile pastime they have to outgrow. And I'm not too fearful the seeming excess of this in American and foreign films these days is likely to corrupt young people or encourage any further loosening of moral restraint. I suspect it is likely to generate an eventual mass monotony, not toward sex but toward these movies about sex. As Samuel Goldwyn once said, "Sex will outlive all of us."

I asked a moment ago how much our movies have informed us and enlightened us about war. How much have they made us sense war's horror, its degradation, dehumanization, and futility? Look at almost any American war film, from *The Big Parade* back in the silent films, to Frank Sinatra's *Van Ryan's Express,* or *The Dirty Dozen,* or John Wayne's *Green Berets,* and you'll see a film that may show you the brutality and the gruesome discomfort of war, but you'll see the fellows you're made to root for as heroes, and you'll be led to have a vicarious satisfaction in their triumphs or in their sacrifice, if they are killed.

Outside of a few films such as the French *La Grande Illusion* and Stanley Kubrick's *The Paths of Glory,* which grimly said that war is madness and the forcing of men into it is folly and injustice of the most inhuman sort, the run of war films is aimed at supporting the popular myth that war may be hell but it is one of those things that good fellows just have to do for their country every now and then.

Right now, of course, we are seeing a lot of war pictures on TV, actual news shots of fellows slogging, fighting, and dying in Vietnam. While this is valid information as to the nature and the anguish of that war, and most of it is presented to make us sense how dismal it is, I feel that the endless repetition of these pictures almost every night tends to numb the nerves and weary the emotions and put the constant viewer into a state of apathy.

What's more, the showing of such pictures right there in the Box, alongside cigarette commercials and serial dramas of the most banal sort, reduces them to the shock importance of, let us say, an automobile collision in *Peyton Place* or the heroic suffering and dying of men in *The Bridge on the River Kawi.* Somehow, I fear the illustration of war in Vietnam merges the reality of that sad conflict with the unreality we safely endure in our war-film myths, and we are not quite sure nor care, in some cases, whether we are seeing the fighting in Saigon or the blowing up of the bridge on the River Kwai.

In short, our war films of the past have not prepared us for revulsion of the war in Vietnam, revulsion of the sort that many young people and many of us older ones have learned from other sources of enlightenment about war.

Neither have movies shown us, except in a few documentaries of late, and in one or two minor feature pictures, the immensity and the tragedy of the long drama of racial injustice that has been occurring in our midst. I can recall a half dozen or so movies that have forcefully dramatized some of the surface aspects of racial conflict and discrimination in the United States. There was *The Defiant Ones,* some years ago, with Tony Curtis and Sidney Poitier as two chain-gang convicts who have escaped and are shackled together so they have to cooperate, even though filled with mutual hate. There was *Intruder in the Dust,* a splendid picture about a white boy saving an elderly Negro from a threatened lynching in the South. There was *Nothing But a Man,* a moving drama of a young Negro husband who can't get a job.

There have been others, but not many, and certainly not enough to illuminate this most cruel and ironic situation in a free society. Nor enough to make us aware of the many natures and the many problems of Negroes, as we have presumably been made aware of whites.

In this connection, I might say that I am happy about the recognition and success that have come to Sidney Poitier as a fine performer, but I am worried about the stereotype of the strong, valiant, never-failing hero that he is being called upon to play. The man he is in *Guess Who's Coming to Dinner,* and even in *In the Heat of the Night,* is but an extension of the sentimental figure he was in *To Sir, With Love* and *A Patch of Blue.* This is again a calculated adjustment to the prevalence of middle-class myth. This is the standard ideal of the Good Negro. Next they'll have Mr. Poitier playing James Bond.

What this shows is the disposition of the average moviegoer to commit himself, to allow for self-improvement, with the attractive or the romantic type. Commitment to the unattractive, to the antisocial or even the psychotic type, is much more difficult and reluctantly extended by American audiences.

There has been no reluctance whatsoever by millions of people to let themselves become involved with the comical, sentimental, juvenile delinquencies of *Bonnie and Clyde*. Two rollicking, fun-loving youngsters who just happen to rob banks and kill people are allowed to be part of the current myth of liberated and just possibly misguided youth. And when these two people are gunned down by the nasty, sadistic police, it is accepted as a poignant demonstration that crime—no matter how unintended—doesn't pay. The taste for Bonnie and Clyde is one of the strangest manifestations of sentiment I have ever seen.

On the other hand, very few people will commit themselves, not even their minds, to the ugly pair of dark, inexplicable murderers that are represented so accurately and relentlessly in the film *In Cold Blood*. Here is a study and a drama that does show us something of the madness in our world, something of the kinds of dangerous people who are running loose, something of the terrifying weaknesses of our protective systems to prevent. This uncomfortable film shows too clearly the aberrant and animalistic nature of too many human beings. As from some of the films of Ingmar Bergman, people turn away from this one in disgust.

Mention of these two pictures brings up a matter that is startlingly conspicuous of great concern to many of us. That is the excess of violence that has been evident in films, the calculated displays of raw aggression, sadism, hurt, and shock.

Oddly enough, there is an artful minimum of actual graphic show of the committing of violence in *In Cold Blood*. The four mad murders are not literally shown, just the events leading up to their occurrence. Thus the imagination is that much more intensely fired.

But there is plenty of bloody, nauseous violence in the playful *Bonnie and Clyde*, and a hideous amount of gruesome sadism in *The Dirty Dozen*, culminating with a roomful of Nazi officers and their women being bathed in burning gasoline. There is torture in a film called *The Penthouse*, vicious cruelty and killing in one called *Point Blank*, terrorism and hurtful tormenting done by two hoodlums aboard a subway train in a little item called *The Incident*, and nice chunks of extra rare violence in any number of other films.

Why this sudden deluge hit us all of a heap some time ago, and is continuing, is not altogether clear to me. It may be because the film makers are always ready to follow a trend. The old motto in this creative business is, as it is in the dress industry, "If at first you do succeed, you keep on doing it until you fail." Well, it may be the trend-following film makers were very much impressed and inspired by the amounts of fantastic, grotesque violence there was in the successful James Bond films, and decided that this sort of stimulation was what the mass audience currently desired.

This is my only explanation for it. And this theory may be supported by other evidences that the public is committing and tolerating other violence in actuality and in myth. Anyhow, the deluge of it in movies, just at this critical time, has been exceedingly unfortunate, to my mind. It is a way of communicating and stimulating violent emotions that has not helped matters in the least.

To be sure, I am not able to prove this, as we never have been able to *prove* that movies alone, or what is in them, primarily inspire behavior patterns and essentially affect our ways of life.

I can only tell you, for instance, that at a showing of *Bonnie and Clyde* in a Broadway theatre, I saw and heard young fellows around me stomping their feet and squealing gleefully when the policemen were shot in the ambush scene and, at the end, when Bonnie and Clyde were mowed down.

Evidently there have been great changes in public values and tolerance of shock in the past few years, and maybe movies have been but reflecting such change. But I wonder whether this is an accurate estimation of the larger public sense of rightness and desirability. I ask whose ox is being gored.

This is a hasty, sketchy survey of what our movie communication is today—that is, in the major, dominant area of the theatrical commercial film. I have not made more than passing mention of minor kinds and uses of films—that is, in the line of documentaries, industrial and educational films.

In these areas, some exceptionally constructive and encouraging things are being done. The device of the motion picture is being employed to make films that shed light, agitate thought, study behavior, and generally educate.

An example of such picture-making is an excellent domumentary called *A Time for Burning*. It is a literal, on-the-spot account of the confusions and reactions in the congregation of a Lutheran church in Omaha when the young minister tried to get his white parishioners to associate on a social and parochial level with members of a Negro Lutheran congregation in the same city.

If you haven't seen this picture, you should see it. It is a startling, devastating, and sad revelation of middle-class behavior in the face of this burning issue of integration and humanity in these difficult times.

But I wouldn't be surprised if you haven't seen it, for its producers have had a difficult time getting distribution for it. It was shown briefly in a commercial theatre in New York, and it has been shown on educational television several times, I believe. It was also up for an Oscar, but it didn't win.

This is an example of the limitation of communication by movies of this sort in our free society.

What of the future? What progress or changes are likely for movies in the years ahead?

The most hopeful prospect for advancement, to my way of viewing it, lies in the expanding areas of interest and exhibition of films in the schools and colleges. The great phenomenon we have seen in the past decade of young people discovering cinema, not as we did when we were youngsters—in the front rows of our neighborhood theatres, watching Tom Mix or Humphrey Bogart —but in the theatres showing foreign films that offer kinds of entertainment and attitudes that are considerably different from those of Hollywood.

It is this growth of student interest, begun in the metropolitan universities and areas, and now spreading to colleges, universities, and high schools all over the United States, that has encouraged the opening of film societies and the distribution of special films— new imports, old imports, and American classics—on hundreds of campuses.

Thus a new appreciation of motion pictures and new values are being spread. Film making is being taught in university courses, and an expanding body of student-made films is now finding circulation on the college circuit. The ferment is intense.

My only concern about it is that it may encourage too many students who use cameras the way dilettantes in the past used paint. In a sense, this surge of excitement about moviemaking by students may be but an extension of elementary school show-and-tell. Students may simply be demonstrating their precocity with movie cameras the way we kids used to demonstrate our precocity with hand printing presses and saxophones.

But I guess that's all right. Out of this, some artful and skillful film makers may emerge. And certainly the appreciation of motion pictures that is being spread is splendid.

Some highly ambitious and esoteric experiments in the usage of films for educating large masses of primitive peoples are being carried on by the National Film Board in Canada. In this sort of thing, and in the possibilities of computer-tape and long-line distribution of education films to school systems all over the country, there are prospects of progress with this medium.

I suspect, too, that the whole system of distributing commercial films in theatres may be radically changed with the ultimate perfection of a system of pay-TV. Feature films in the home—*without commercials* and with higher production qualities—could be the next big move of magic to shake up the inevitable slump into the next phase of monotony.

But this, of course, is likely to bring upon us the burden that has not been fully shed—that is, the burden of control of film content by some statutory agency. The present threat is what is called classification, the idea of judging and grading films as to their suitability for children. And this is but another way to impose the tastes of the middle-class preceptors and their censors on a free society.

I cannot be as brightly optimistic about the overall improvement of movie culture as some persons may be about the press. I know that the big periods of expanding energy in the content of films have come only after great and even calamitous crises in human affairs.

Perhaps we may have to undergo some terrible passage through a valley of social strife, some further upheaval, before we or our children witness an essential change in the culture of films.

And yet I continue to go to movies, to study and indeed enjoy them, even when I may be sitting there steaming at something in them that causes pain.

Perhaps I am like the husband of the lady my wife overheard talking to another lady in a beauty parlor one day. The other lady had asked her friend whether she had seen the film called *God Created Woman*, which was showing just at that time. *God Created Woman*, you may remember, was a sensational French film with Brigitte Bardot, and it was of such a nature that there wasn't any question that its principal character *was* a woman. "No, I haven't seen it," said the lady. "But my husband saw it the other day in New York. And he was shocked by it, absolutely shocked. Indeed, he was not only shocked the first time he saw it, but he was shocked the *second* time, too!"

Well, I'm sure we'll all keep on going to movies, and I daresay we'll keep on being shocked.